Harriet Schott '92

℞ For Adventure

℞ For Adventure: Bush Pilot Doctor

by Elmer E. Gaede
with Naomi Gaede-Penner

Great Northwest Publishing
and Distributing Company, Inc.
Anchorage, Alaska
1991

Copyright © 1991 by Naomi Gaede-Penner
ALL RIGHTS RESERVED
ISBN 0-937708-35-6
Printed in the United States of America
First Edition 1991

DEDICATION

Dedicated to my husband, Bryan G. Penner, who exuberantly loved life, flying and hunting; and who cheered me on in writing this book—yet didn't live to see its completion.

ACKNOWLEDGMENTS

My deep appreciation to Pat Quigley who encouraged me to be a writer and who graciously critiques everything I write.

CONTENTS

Introduction		ix
Foreword		xi
Chapter 1	Opening the door to the last frontier	1
Chapter 2	Tundra taxi	10
Chapter 3	Flying or bust!	18
Chapter 4	The Thanksgiving Day moose	24
Chapter 5	Lime Village evacuation	32
Chapter 6	Out to get a bear rug	40
Chapter 7	Assignment: Tanana	49
Chapter 8	A strange village welcome	56
Chapter 9	House calls Alaskan style	62
Chapter 10	King of the Arctic	70
Chapter 11	Break-up takeoff	82
Chapter 12	Hunting: Not for men only	89
Chapter 13	Close encounters of many kinds	97
Chapter 14	Tooth-pullin' time	103
Chapter 15	Double-feature drama	107
Chapter 16	The last Alaskan nomads	112
Chapter 17	℞ for excitement: Mix flying with medicine	119
Chapter 18	The top of Alaska	126
Chapter 19	Back home	139
Chapter 20	The day the earth broke apart	150
Chapter 21	Return to Point Hope	157
Chapter 22	Flight by faith	167
Chapter 23	No ordinary day	173
Chapter 24	The Valley of 10,000 Smokes revisited	179

INTRODUCTION
By Naomi Gaede-Penner

His hospital ward included twenty-two villages edged along the mighty Yukon River; his ambulance was a red Family Cruiser airplane. What persuaded him to exchange the rolling, golden wheatfields of Kansas for the disolate tundra and formidable mountains of the Yukon Territory? The lure of gold was not the attraction, but the age-old challenge of man against nature grabbed at his indomitable, adventure-seeking spirit. This quest, along with his love and respect for the Native people, has held him to Alaska for over thirty years.

"Doc," as Dr. Elmer E. Gaede has been called over his years of medical missionary work in Alaska, headed up the Alcan Highway with his family to Anchorage in 1955. Here he stepped in beside other living legends such as Noel Wien, pioneer for Alaskan commercial aviation; Don Sheldon, bush pilot for Mt. McKinley expeditions; Don Stickman, native bush pilot; and John Chambers, missionary bush pilot.

No sooner had Doc washed "Alaska or Bust" off his dusty Chevy when he realized that Anchorage was only a door to

Alaska and that the dead-end roads of Alaska prevented him from entering into "real" Alaska—the bush. The ticket for further passage came in the form of flying lessons with a fragile, Christmas-tree colored J-3 on floats. This second achievement propelled him into a series of heart-warming, never-ending adventures.

The following pages show the personal, and often humorous account of a man's growth from a novice attempting to deal with the rigors of the Last Frontier, to a man worthy of the title "Bush Pilot Doctor." Each chapter in this book is a complete action-packed story of flying, medicine, or hunting; from downing a 2000 pound moose, to cracking up his plane—several times, to acquiring self-taught dentistry skills, to hanging onto a psychotic patient who tries to bail out of the plane—2000 feet above the Yukon, to carrying an Eskimo baby back to its home. Here are stories not only for men and boys who want a hero, but for fun family reading as well.

FOREWORD

An "experience" is something that while it is happening to you, you wish it was happening to someone else. In this book we have just those exciting experiences that happen to someone else while we sit back in a comfortable chair and enjoy the dilemma. These experiences were a result of the lure of Alaska and the lure of flying tugging at a Kansas boy who took his first airplane ride at a county fair at age 15.

With a dedication to serve his God and fellow human beings, he first became a doctor. Then, with a finger writing on the hump-back of his dusty Chevy, "Alaska or Bust," he and his family trekked up the Alaska-Canada Highway to serve a two year assignment at the Alaska Native Hospital in Anchorage.

Next it was time to answer the lure of flying. The slogan changed to "Flying or Bust." Here starts the tale of experiences covering some thirty-five years as a doctor and bush pilot in our Last Frontier.

I came to Alaska in 1939 as a pilot. I didn't know that I was making history so I kept no record. We are indeed fortunate that Doc Gaede did, thus giving us history in the raw as we thrill with those experiences where he answered his calling to serve God and the men and women in Alaska.

There's an adage many of us Alaskan pilots were brought up on: "There are old pilots and there are bold pilots, but there are no old, bold pilots." Most of us longtime surviving bush pilots had to infringe on that. Doc Gaede infringed on it so much we have to label him a "violator of the first order." But now, as you'll see, we have to forgive him those violations as over time and time again he responded to necessity.

Sit back. Fasten your seatbelts. Enjoy the experience.

Fred Chambers
Retired American Airline Captain
Missionary Pilot

1
Opening the door to the last frontier
1955

"Daddy, what is a mountain?"

I could almost hear my little daughter's question from the year before as I sat in the doctor's lounge one evening at the Anchorage Alaska Native Service (ANS) Hospital, waiting for the next emergency. My introduction to mountains and Alaska had come the previous summer, July 1955, when my wife, Ruby, and our two preschoolers, Naomi and Ruth, journeyed for eight days from Kansas to the Alaskan Territory.

Like a broken record my five-year-old daughter, Naomi, queried me from her standing-on-her-head position beside her younger sister in the back seat of our once-shiny black '47 Fleetline Chevy: "What is a mountain?" The only "mountains" we knew were the rolling hills of the Kansas University campus at Lawrence, where I had completed medical school.

Even though I came from a farming background, I didn't see a future in dairy farming. Besides that, I was fascinated by the medical careers of several of my relatives. Consequently, I changed from a farm boy milking dairy cows to a medical doctor treating people. At age 32, I had a new certificate that boldly asserted: "Elmer E. Gaede, M.D."

For me, medical work and missionary work seemed to go hand in hand. Originally I intended to be a medical missionary in South America, but at that time there were no openings with the Mennonite Brethren Missions Board, under which I wanted to serve. One option was to wait. I couldn't wait. If I could not officially be a missionary doctor, I felt sure I could make my profession into a mission in some untamed setting. I headed north—to Alaska.

Why did I chose the frozen tundra, rather than the torrid jungles? What had influenced my drastic turn about? An exuberant nurse, working with me during my residency at Bethany Hospital in Kansas City, had inundated me with exciting stories of medical possibilities in Alaska. She had worked at the hospital in Bethel, Alaska, for several years, and even now continued to correspond with friends who remained there. "It's a door to opportunities!"

As I investigated these opportunities, I learned that the Bureau of Indian Affairs (BIA) was being replaced by the United States Public Health Service (PHS). Consequently the Alaskan Native hospitals needed additional medical officers. Furthermore, the doctor-draft law would allow my work there to qualify as government service, and thus I could fulfill my impending military obligations. In addition, we'd heard that there was good money as a physician with Public Health— maybe even $7,000 to $9,000 a year.

I requested employment at the Anchorage ANS Hospital. Request granted. The door swung open to the Last Frontier.

Edging toward that door, the snail-shaped Chevy crept along, much too slowly for our eagerness. At last we saw not only *a* mountain, but rows of jagged majestic mountains. The steep roads through the northern Rocky Mountain ranges challenged the tired Chevy, but, when we arrived at their peaks, we were usually treated to a dusty, yet awe-inspiring wonderland where the winter snowbanks, hollowed out by the summer's warmth, formed dripping, blue-shadowed snow caves beside the road for us to explore.

At Dawson Creek, we got acquainted with the chuck-holed Alcan Highway. No small engineering feat, the highway resolutely trudged over permafrost, muskeg, spagnum moss, and thousand-foot canyons. Primarily constructed as a military supply route to Alaska for U.S. forces, the Alaska-Canada Military Highway was opened to the public in 1948 after the Canadians felt assured that there were adequate gas stations and lodging for travelers. The Alcan extended through the Yukon Territory to Fairbanks, Alaska.

We ploughed up this dust-choked highway, and finally, after "Alaska or Bust" had repeatedly been finger-written on the dirty hump of the Chevy and Ruby and I had our ears filled with the girls's, "Are we there yet?" we arrived outside of Anchorage.

Later we were told of the discussion that arose over this city's name. *Woodrow Creek* for President Woodrow Wilson was one option. Other people suggested *Whitney* and *Brownsville* for two early homesteaders. None of these names actually appeared on the ballot, but instead nine other names were listed, among them *Matanuska, Gateway, Ship Creek and Anchorage. Anchorage* won by an overwhelming majority since the name accurately described the site, which was an anchorage for boats that brought freight to the railroad and the coal mines.

Now as we were about to become residents of this city, we were tired of dust, and so at our trail's end we decided to clean up. Before driving into Anchorage, we stopped to camp at Ship Creek, a wonderfully clean, clear river, where we could clean up and wash the dust off the Chevy.

The next evening as we drove into Anchorage, we wondered about the strange haze over the city. Then we noticed our black car reverting back to a sooty gray. We were wrong about the city bringing relief from the dust. Dust spun up under our tires from the gravel roads, which ran among dilapidated buildings, sod-roofed log cabins, and modern housing developments, and settled on scattered pink wild roses and indigo wildflowers.

The only roads paved were the highway, and 5th, 6th, 9th, and Gambell streets, although there were sidewalks downtown and in some housing developments. We quickly learned, and agreed with the standing joke: "Welcome to Anchorage. Bump. Bump. Bump."

Not knowing where to establish "home," we checked into the North Star Motel on Gambell Street. Here the clerk made Naomi and Ruth feel at home, gifting them with occasional nickels for an ice cream across the street. In the evenings we usually went out to eat—by the river at Ship Creek flats, at Lake Spenard, or along Turnagain Arm. Ruby, a true pioneer, fought kamikaze mosquitos and cooked hot dogs and canned soups over a campfire. I either washed the car, a futile job, or talked with other campers,—a mix of tourists and summer workers, some of whom lived in their cars.

"Daddy, isn't Alaska great?" said Naomi one evening, as she and Ruth clunked rocks into the clear rushing water.

"Yes," I answered. "And I bet it's going to get even better."

Ruby, however, did not immediately share my enthusiasm. "Elmer, this is so different from Kansas." she said, while skillfully stoking the fire without dislodging the frying pan. "The waving wheatfields were so open and spacious. Now, here we are trapped with mountains to the east and water to the south and west."

No, these purple mountain majesties and silver shining sea were not like the vast expanse of Kansas golden fields of grain. I thought of how this territory attracted some people, while creating uneasiness in others. I hoped Ruby would soon grow more comfortable here.

"There is only one real way out of here back to civilization. What would happen if that road were ever cut off?" she said, rubbing campfire smoke out of her hazel eyes and trying to shake a mosquito out of her shiny brown hair.

Instead of speaking to her hemmed-in feelings, I changed the subject. Pointing to a large rock near our campfire, and on which both Naomi and Ruth both tried to perch, I said. "I wonder who has sat right here, in years before us? If the rock could talk, I bet it would tell us tales of history."

Back in the early 1900s when Alaska needed transportation from interior coal fields to exterior waterways, Alaska's railway system was just beginning. Although originally planned for Seward, Anchorage was selected for the headquarters. Word of the new railroad created a kind of construction worker's gold rush. To assist in the construction, nearly 2,000 people rushed up from the states, pitching tents on these same flats.

In the summer of 1915, the tent city was ordered to move. At the same time, lots were auctioned off on the south ledge overlooking Cook Inlet. Anchorage was born.

We moved, too—from living in the motel to 16th Street in City View, a new residential area on the outskirts of town. Facing the west, our large living room window offered us a panoramic view. During the summer and fall, three-foot-high pink fireweed burst out along the road against the backdrop of the Alaskan Range. Within this range rested a shapely section appropriately named *Sleeping Lady*. At times she lay blanketed with puffy white clouds, and during the late summer evenings golden lavender rays covered her.

In winter the pink flower hues were exchanged for the pink glow of frozen sun on subzero snow. On a clear day, we could look toward the north and see Alaska's centerpiece: the eternally snow-cloaked Mt. McKinley, her head held high and poking through a wreath of clouds. Dog sleds mushed across our view, interrupting the still life.

Whenever I had time off, we explored our new habitat. Often, our excursions were short and included summer picnics, or fall blueberry picking in rustcolored swamps with white fluffy pompons of wild cotton grass, or red cranberry picking among white birch trees with falling toasted-orange leaves. The "fruits" seemed strange and tart since we were used to sweet peaches and apricots.

On other occasions we ventured farther. For instance, in late summer, we drove around the Knik Arm through the Matanuska Valley to Valdez. At the Arm, an entire field of shooting stars threw out a welcome mat and smiled with little black and white faces, surrounded by fushia ruffles. Ruby loved them and the showy blue lupines with wandlike clusters, which joined the abundant magenta fireweed along the highway.

We'd heard Paul Bunyan tales of the farming in the Matanuska Valley, which was an experiment emerging out of the Great Depression and carried on under the auspices of the Alaska Rural Rehabilitation Corporation. In 1935, social workers selected 203 families of hardy Scandinavian descent from Michigan, Minnesota, and Wisconsin to establish farms. The farms, nurtured by the sheltering Talkeetna mountains to the north, fertile soil, and Alaska's around-the-clock sunlight, produced abundantly.

The State Fair there, in Palmer, erased any doubts we had about the stories: seventy-pound cabbages, radishes the length of a hand, and cauliflower the size of a basketball.

Our next point of interest on our way to Valdez was Worthington Glacier, on the Richardson Highway near Thompson Pass. There we cranked homemade ice cream. Ruby had planned ahead and packed the freezer with ingredients into the car trunk. Making homemade ice cream at glaciers later became a family tradition. Before continuing on, we walked and slipped on top of the glacier, holding our breath as we jumped across two-foot-wide cravasses and then peered down into their bottomless turquoise depths.

To get to our destination, we drove through the rugged Alplike Chugach Mountains. Smudges of clouds grouped together and cut off their peaks, then ran away, leaving sharp outlines against the royal blue sky. Pocketed against this spectacular background and embraced by the nearby Valdez glacier, the town pointed toward Prince William Sound, with houses and log cabins scattered along two gravel streets. Only a few boats contentedly rocked along the short dock, which jutted out from another street running alongside the waterfront.

Often called Alaska's "Little Switzerland," Valdez was discovered in 1790 by a Spanish explorer and subsequently received its Spanish name. In 1897, thousands of gold seekers bound for the Klondike gold fields stampeded to this mostnortherly ice-free port.

These facts, which I liked to collect and then share with my family, did not impress Ruth and Naomi as much as the enormous wild raspberries beside the road on the edge of the town. They were entranced by the frothy waterfalls, some frolicking gently down the mountainside with angel-hair spray, nearly hidden by the towering dark green spruce. Others demanded to be noticed as they pounded their way into view with a deafening roar.

At Crooked Creek, we watched the determined, sickly, spawning salmon, torn by rocks, exhausted by jumping, coming to the end of their journey. "We, too, are once again at the end of a road, with only one way out," mused Ruby. "How do people survive at this end of the world, much less enjoy it—I couldn't live here, pressed in between the water and the mountains, which are so tall and dark they seem to almost lean over on us."

Being an optimist, I interpreted that comment to mean Ruby was adjusting to our new home and that Anchorage did seem civilized and almost spacious in contrast to Valdez.

The smiling face of the "Land of the Midnight Sun" showed its cold back as the summer abruptly ended with frost in August and snow in September. In the early days, when the only transportation between Alaska and the United States was by ship, the signal for the summer workers to head south before freeze-up were these first snows, which came to about the 3000-foot level. *Termination dust,* the snows were appropriated called.

In February, I wrote home to my uncle in California that, "We are having about twice as bad weather as we get in Kansas. Yesterday and today we have winds up to 55 mph, and the streets are drifting closed every fifteen to thirty minutes. I suppose the mayor will declare an emergency again and close business tomorrow."

That blizzard shrieked around us, pounding the doors and windows, not stopping until snow piled up to the roof on the south side of our house. Outside, road graders attempted to clear the streets, and snowblowers swallowed up the ubiquitous white stuff, spewing it out in soft, puffy ribbons.

On Saturday and Sunday afternoons, we discovered nature's winter amusement park nearly in our front yard. Across the road was a skating area and then a half block west the 30- to 40-foot high gravel pit hills supplied great sledding and tobogganing fun.

The Anchorage Fur Rendezvous, held in February, provided more entertainment. Originally a celebration when trappers came to sell their winter's cache of furs, this annual, 10-day cabin-fever antidote attracted crowds of Natives and whites. The hustle and bustle of dogsled races, dog-pull contests, snow-shoe races, and fur auctions nearly shut down 5th Street. In one of the open lots there was a platform with hundreds of raw furs, sectioned off for red fox, white fox, mink, beaver, muskrat, lynx, and wolverine.

At the first of the Rendevous, I bid on the red fox and got two for $5 each. The next day, some of the same quality of fox went up to $20 each. I was told that I did well to bid early since the furs usually sell low the first few days before the buying interest is up. Later, when the buying "fever" is aroused, the prices go up.

The odor went up later, too, when the furs were brought in from the cold and into a warm room. Some of the furs came from villages where they had been tanned in barrels of human urine. I learned that in fur selection, one needed to use both eyes and nose.

"Dr. Gaede," a nurse spoke to me from the lounge door, interupting my silent reminiscing. "A hunting accident is coming in. A man shot himself in the foot." Walking down the hall to the emergency room, I heard another nurse's voice echoing in my mind—the nurse who had first sparked my interest in Alaska.—"opportunity!"

Seven of us medical officers had been assigned to develop the various departments of the 400-bed hospital. This Anchorage ANS Hospital, recently opened on November 29, 1953, was one of eight ANS hospitals in Alaska. The six-story structure, dominating the skyline in the eastern part of the city, was designed in the shape of a cross, with a solarium on the sixth floor that at the time offered one of the most spectacular views of Cook Inlet and the Chugach Range.

With all the needs in the hospital, there was some choice as to work preference, and my roles were multiple. Anethesia was one choice since I had just finished my intership in this area. In addition, since none of the other officers was interested in obstetrics, I also became Chief of Obstetrics. The native women commonly had 12 to 15 pregnancies, and the Eskimos especially had easy deliveries. Chief of Outpatients rounded out my list of duties.

My patients, Indian, Aleut, and Eskimo provided many opportunities to learn about the Native people, their ways of life, customs, and hardships. Often I would relate these stories to my family around the supper table.

As with other American Indians, infant mortality rate among the Alaskan Natives was very high. For Alaskan infants, the rate was three times that for white infants. Some of this was due to pneumonia, early infancy diseases, and accidents. During the past several years, chiefs had begun sending their wives to the hospital, rather than using the traditional village midwifery to deliver their babies.

The typical two-week hospitalization by mother and baby

gave the babies an extra boost before reentering village life. While in the hospital, birth defects, especially heart defects, could be detected. During the stay, the mothers were taught infant care. When mother and baby did return home, canned milk and vitamins were sent along for the babies.

In December of 1956, when our son, Mark, was born in the Anchorage ANS Hospital, Ruby shared her room with a chief's wife from Savoonga on St. Lawrence Island.

"You should see the contrast between your new brother and the Eskimo baby," I told Naomi and Ruth. "The Native baby is long and thin, and has lots of thick black hair. Mark is chubby, pale white—and bald." To illustrate the point further, I lined up all the babies in the nursery, including Mark, and took a picture.

The St. Lawrence Island Eskimos were well known for their finely detailed ivory carving. In exchange for a healthy son, the chief, who did not speak English, generously and gratefully opened up his seal-skin bag, allowing me to choose gifts. I deliberated. The decision was not easy. Finally I settled on an ivory owl, an ivory bracelet for Ruby, and a fertility stick:—a long piece of ivory, etched with Alaskan scenes. These I added to my small collection of ivory salt and pepper shakers, soft fur and skin Eskimo yo-yos, and miniature skin kayaks.

The Natives' kindness touched me, and I wanted to learn more about them and their great land. There was so much more out there that I had not seen. I did what I could, volunteering for medical emergency missions to remote villages, but that was not enough. Something had grabbed hold of me. It was like . . .

"Dr. Gaede? What is *frontier fever*?" The emergency room nurse was giving a strange look as I scrubbed for the shooting accident. I guess I'd spoken my thoughts out loud.

"Oh, it's a malady cheechakos sometimes get," I stammered, a little embarrassed. "I hear the prognosis isn't good and some individuals have even had to be quarantined in Alaska for the rest of their lives."

I had a funny feeling that maybe I'd contracted that disease—hopefully I'd someday accumulate stories and be able to tell others about this great land of opportunity. But to do that, I'd have to explore more of Alaska.

2
Tundra taxi
February 1956

Cradling the newborn baby in the crook of my arm and carrying a diaper bag, I climbed on board the DC 3 and looked around for a seat. No seat assignments. No flight attendants. Besides the flight crew, myself, and the two-week-old baby, I counted only five Eskimo men. Crates, machinery parts, ropes, construction supplies, and other cargo had crowded ahead of us and now occupied seats and floor space. The air was thick with the smell of oily tarpaulines.

"Be glad this plane has a few seats left," said the pilot, a dark, bearded man filling up the cockpit door. "Try to find one with seatbelts."

I exchanged greetings with the other passengers. "This is Andrew." I said, gently patting my layered bundle. They smiled curiously, but politely asked nothing, then together we checked the seats for seatbelts. After a few minutes, I managed to locate not only a seat with a belt, but a seat with a window view. This was my first experience heading into the Interior, and now I was going to see the "real" Alaska. I wasn't sure what to expect, but I didn't want to miss anything. Maybe one of the Eskimo men could tell me about Noatak—where I was headed. I looked around. Unfortunately, no one sat near me.

I settled into my seat and buckled in. The giant propellors reluctantly ground to a start in the $-40°$ F Fairbank's air. The baby, undisturbed by the commotion and the cold, continued to sleep in my arms.

This was the second leg of our trip. Several hours ago, at 9:30 A.M., and just as the February sun was weakly dawning, my small companion and I boarded a DC 4 and set out on our 750-mile journey, which zigzagged from Anchorage International Airport, north to Fairbanks, west to Kotzebue, and then to the baby's home in the village of Noatak.

Getting anywhere in winter took a long time and in 1956 the flights were few and far between. People agreed to fly in anything. Now I was finding out that when heading into the Interior there was no distinction between cargo and passenger planes. Nonetheless, things weren't as grim as in earlier years, such as in 1942, when the flight between Fairbanks and Nome took six hours with a rest stop about halfway at Galena.

I was traveling with the baby because his mother had tuberculosis and needed to remain in the Anchorage ANS Hospital for an indefinite period of time. That year, when the Public Health Service took over the Bureau of Indian Affairs, they discovered an appalling proportion of tuberculosis among the Natives.

Instead of the typically less than 80 per 100,000 number of cases in the general U.S. population, the Alaskan Native's cases were 2,300 per 100,000.

It was not uncommon for the pregnant Native woman to come into the hospital for delivery, be diagnosed as having tuburculosis, and end up staying in the hospital while their babies went home to be with the other family members. In many cases, family or friends would come get the baby. When this was not possible, one of the hospital medical personnel served as baby courier.

I chuckled to myself. Little did I know when I'd taken the job at the ANS Hospital, that "baby escort service" was written between the lines of my contract. Actually, I'd volunteered for this opportunity so I could venture outside of Anchorage and "really see Alaska."

Andrew whimpered as the plane lurched off the airstrip and into the stiff air. I pulled back the blue flannel blanket, which protected his face from the raw air. Thick black hair crowded around his face. His dark almond eyes searched mine and then responded with a cry. As a father of three young children, I was acquainted with babies. When the baby continued to complain, I suspected the usual—a wet diaper. Seeing my breath in the frigid cabin, I decided for the baby's benefit to wait until the temperature rose to expose him to the cold. Nevertheless, thirty minutes later, I still shivered in the frosty cabin, and the baby cried unrelentingly.

"Can we expect cabin heat soon?" I walked up to the cockpit and inquired.

"Seems there's a problem with heat out there." answered the copilot matter-of-factly. "Hope you have enough clothes on."

Wishing for better accommodations, I returned to my seat, and hastily changed the baby. "There, there." I said in my most soothing voice. "I know this isn't fun. I'm hurrying as fast as I can."

He offered me no forgiveness—or silence. His cries intensified. Now what? I dug around for his bottle. Giving it the milk-drop-on-wrist test, I knew he would be angrier yet with the Yukon-cold liquid.

The cockpit had heat, I wondered if we could at least get the chill out of this milk by placing it beside the heater. Once again I walked up the aisle and apologetically explained my plight to the crew.

Sure enough, within twenty minutes the copilot brought back a hot meal for the baby—something the rest of us could have used by this time.

Finally satisfied, the baby slept for the rest of the trip. I scraped the reappearing frost off my window. This was a great opportunity to see Alaska. Now where were we? I pulled a map out of my pocket and tried to identify landmarks. What had I missed so far?

From this aerial perspective, I could understand why the

Territory had been misunderstood as a refrigerated wasteland. There wasn't much to see— especially in winter with the perpetual snow, long winter nights, and powerful cold that plunged to record-holding −80° F.

I located Kotzebue on my map and finger-traced a line from Fairbanks, trying to determine our location. I'd read all about Kotzebue and its population of over 80 percent Eskimo. Kititagruk, as it was called then, was accidently discovered in 1816 by a Polish explorer, Otto von Kotzebue, who was in the service of Russia and looking for the Northwest Passage. What interested me more was that Kotzebue was known as the Polar Bear capital of the world. Wouldn't that be exciting to shoot one of those arctic kings? My mind wandered around in possibilities, just as the rivers wandered around the black-on-white tree-studded terrain below me.

After two hours, the plane circled Kotzebue, then landed a mile south of the village. Holding the baby tightly, I waited for the plane steps to be let down. Then peering into the 2:00 P.M. dusk, I cautiously stepped out into the Arctic air.

"How do we get to the village?" I started to ask one of the men, but the fierce wind with a chill factor of more than minus −60° F rudely whipped my wolf parka ruff into my face and snatched away my words, leaving my frozen lips without any desire to repeat the question.

Ahead of me, the Eskimo men soundlessly padded across the blowing snow in their mukluked feet. Where were they going? My white felt-topped army "bunny boots" crunched and slid along after the group. There was no terminal building. I needed to get to the satellite ANS Hospital in the village a mile away. Would the baby stay warm out here? How far could we walk in this ice box? Not finding any other options, I hurried to catch up with the men in front of me.

So this was the Interior. Formidable. Instead of a warm handshake to welcome me, the arctic wind grabbed me, and crept through my heavy army parka and wool army pants, past my insulated underwear, and straight to my bones. Meanwhile, the baby slept. "He had better get used to this." I mused. "This is home."

As I tagged along, a small rectangular shed appeared. I followed the men through the door, where I could make out wooden shelves which extended along two walls. Copying the others, I sat down and looked around. They seemed to be waiting for something—waiting with assurance and anticipation that something was going to happen.

"We will go to the village soon," one man informed me. At least the bodies in the approximately eight-by-twelve shed should soon make some collective heat, I reasoned.

Before long, I heard a chugging sound. Was it a diesel caterpillar tractor? The laboring sound continued, growing louder. Was it going to hit us? The shed began to shake. When would it stop? Maybe it couldn't see us in the blowing snow. I looked around at the others in the shed. They seemed unalarmed. I tried to adopt their casual spirit and act calm, but when the shed suddenly shuttered, I jumped up, which did me no good since the one small window was near the eight-foot ceiling and too high to see out.

The Natives looked at me and then at one another. Andrew cried out his protest. The shed jolted again. At last, one man offered me the puzzle piece I needed. "Cat hooks to shed. Shed has runners—like a sled. Now we go to village."

Sure enough, the shed jerked. I abruptly sat down. In my haste to seek shelter from the cold, I hadn't noticed the runners on this tundra taxi.

The rumble of the Cat put Andrew back to sleep as we crawled along at about 5 mph. I knew the hospital was a mile away and wondered how I should notify the driver of my destination. Even without a pull cord, the Cat driver seemed to know where his other passengers needed to get off. After several stops, the Cat stopped and all was silent. Now what?

The fur-hooded driver poked his head in the door. "Everyone out. This is the end of the route."

Right outside the door was the rambling one-story hospital. What better service could I have asked for? It wasn't until I was inside the welcome warmth that I realized I had never paid or tipped my tundra taxi Cat driver.

Once I'd introduced myself to the smiling woman at the front desk, two nurses immediately appeared. "We've been expecting you—and the baby," said the one with a name tag reading "Mildred," taking Andrew out of my arms.

"Yes, his father and the rest of the relatives can't wait to see him," said her companion. "We'll notify the village right away."

Side by side the nurses proceeded down the hall—with Andrew. My arms felt empty. After all, together Andrew and I had braved wet diapers, cold milk, and the harrowing experience of a tundra taxi.

Reaching out and patting my arm, the desk clerk added, "And, we'll arrange for a charter to fly you to Noatok tomorrow morning," which reminded me that our camaraderie had not yet ended.

As I waited in the lounge for Dr. Rabeau, director of the 55-bed hospital, I looked out the window. Nearby, several dog sleds mushed in from the Kotzebue Sound. They were carrying what appeared to be small logs of firewood. How peculiar. This was above the Arctic Circle where I'd heard that only tundra thrives and stunted bushes survive. Where were they finding this wood?

Mildred walked in, assuring me that Andrew was fine and informing me that Dr. Rabeau would soon arrive. "Where are the Natives getting the wood?" I asked, pointing out the window.

"That's not wood, Dr. Gaede." she chuckled. "Those are frozen shee fish that they've caught through the ice. They weight from 20 to 40 pounds and make excellent eating."

Just then, the heavy-set, white-jacketed Dr. Rabeau entered. "Hello, Elmer. I imagine you've had quite a day. Won't you join me for dinner and then I'll give you a tour of this place."

It had been a long day, but the hot meal restoked my energy—and my curiosity. "Tell me about Noatok."

"It's about 50 miles north of here—about 25 miles inland from the Bering Strait, a small Eskimo village along the Noatok River with about 40 to 50 people," Dr. Rabou explained in his gruff voice.

The following morning, ice fog hung like a sheet over Kotzebue. Frost formed furry sleeves over the skinny bushes and electric lines, etched intricate designs on the window glass, and frosted the edges of all buildings. Even though the wind, which had chased snow around the village during night, had run away, the foggy cold stubbornly refused to leave.

"How do people make it up here?" I wondered as I sipped hot tea in the hospital cafeteria, waiting for information about the last leg of my journey. "They must be a hardy and resourceful lot."

Shortly after noon, the charter pilot, Tommy, sent word that he thought he could take off and make it to Noatok. Instead of taking off from the airstrip from where we had landed, he had his plane tied down on the shore ice a few blocks from the hospital.

Tommy, an Eskimo in his mid-30s, cordially greeted us at the airstrip. The hospital personnel had spoken highly of this friendly, wirey-built Eskimo, and I looked forward to flying with him in his tail-dragging Pacer. I was curious about flying and was considering taking lessons myself, so whenever I encountered pilots, I plied them with questions, such as "What's the best plane to land in the bush? What are "tail-draggers?" Pilots never seemed to tire of plane talk, so my questions were usually not only answered, but accompanied by stories. Without relating all those stories, the consensus was that planes with a back wheel, as contrasted with a nose wheel, were easier to land, could handle more abuse, and therefore provided more stability on rough or uncertain terrain—such as river ice, sandbars, beaches, and so on.

Andrew and I were the only passengers in the four-place plane. I eagerly climbed in beside Tommy. He was a *real* bush pilot, and here was another opportunity to find out more about Alaska. Tommy kept his comments short as he followed the Noatok River, scrutinizing the monochromatic treeless terrain below which blended into the dull sky above.

After awhile, we circled and buzzed what seemed to be just another group of scattered dark spots pressed into the constantly blowing snow, but which turned out to be Noatok. At the sound of the plane, the villagers poured out of their snow-buried sod houses like ants out of a disturbed anthill. On our approach we could see them race toward a smooth area, which seemed to be the designated "airstrip."

Andrew's father, a big grin across his face, was easy to spot. He and the other family members crowded around the plane, passing Andrew around, laughing, and asking questions about the baby's mother. Tommy seemed to know everyone so he joined in the conversation as well.

All too soon, Tommy interrupted the joyous reunion. "Doctor, we've got to get back. There's not much daylight left and if the fog rolls back in we'll never find home. Besides, we don't dare let this engine cool down or we won't get it started."

Andrew's father repeatedly shook my hand, and then, mission accomplished, I patted Andrew and swung up beside Tommy. Yelling "clear prop," Tommy started the engine, and the villagers moved away, smiling and waving. I'd only had a few minutes with those people, but it was as if we were instant friends. I hated to leave.

Tommy adeptly found his way back to Kotzebue, which was no surprise to me since I knew he was one of those invincible bush pilots.

The trip back to Anchorage was eventful in that there was cabin heat. I was thankful for simple things at this point.

Ruby and the children met me at the Merrill Field Airport. Ruth clung to Ruby's hand, Mark wiggled in my arms, and Naomi jumped up and down beside me, asking me questions. "Did you see polar bear? Did you sleep in an igloo?"

"How did the baby do?" asked Ruby.

"No problem." I answered brusquely. I wanted to tell them how one tiny life had touched me and had opened up a new world. Instead I said, "You wouldn't believe the complimentary transportation from the airport!"

Before we crossed the street to the parking lot, a taxi pulled up in front of us and a woman with a baby cradled in her arms climbed in. Smoothly, the taxi pulled away from the curb and drove out of sight in the early afternoon dusk. What a contrast to my experiences the day before.

This trip to the interior only fueled my Alaskan Fever. I had to find a way to get back into territory unreached by roads.

3
Flying or bust!
Spring 1956

"Hey, Doc, you'd love flying." said Wally Zimmer, an enthusiastic friend as we drove away from Lake Hood where his four-place Stinson on floats was anchored to barrel tie-downs.

I was a frequent admirer of the planes that lined the lake. In fact, at this time, the great colorful brood reportedly represented 20 percent of the nation's floatplanes, which meant Lake Hood harbored more floatplanes than any other spot in the world. And no wonder, Alaskans flew approximately thirty times more per capita than the lower 48 residents.

After only a year in this Territory with virtually insurmountable terrain, I could see why. Airplanes meant much more than optional transportation. Vital supplies were carried via air frieght. Emergency aid, more often than not, had to be flown in. The Lower 48 depended on its web of roads and coast-to-coast railway system, while Alaska looked to the skies. "You could *really* see Alaska if you'd learn to fly!" Wally continued, his voice growing louder so as to be heard above the clattered gravel on the narrow two-lane road. I agreed. Just living in Anchorage was not enough. Since the main roads out of Anchorage either dead-ended in Homer on the Kenai Peninsula, or in Fairbanks, flying certainly played a major part in transportation and sightseeing to the majority of the state.

"You know, Doc, a J-3 would be perfect for you! It's economical, a good plane to train on, you wouldn't have any trouble selling it—and a good resale price, too. Even if you'd decide to keep it, it would be a great plane for hunting because of its slow speed." His sales pitch was convincing.

Back home, his words echoed in my mind. I thought of my flight with Tommy to Noatak and remembered the feeling of independence and the sense of defiance of man against nature.

Yes, it did seem like both a sensible thing to do: buy a floatplane and learn to fly. "Alaska or Bust" had become "Flying or Bust" as I looked at another door of opportunity and excitement.

I took a rain check to join the ranks of pilots since the invitation had come in winter when the floatplanes exchanged their floats for skis. The winter in waiting was not wasted since I worked on two projects. First, I devoured everything I could find about Alaskan aviation. Among the bits and pieces of trivia, I found that the first flight in Alaska took place on July 4, 1913, when The Aerial Circus, with James Martin, traveled to the tiny log-cabin settlement of Fairbanks. A crowd watched the dusty take-off of the biplane from the ballpark that stamped a benchmark in Alaskan history.

Ten years later, Ben Eielson, a quiet North Dakota school teacher, not only took off from the same ballpark, but broke a trail across the immeasureable skies of the untamed land, penetrating the air with the never-heard-of-before drone of an aircraft engine. As the first pilot to cross the top of the world, he established airmail service in Alaska and opened the gates of the remote wilderness to commercial and passenger aviation.

The second project: persuading my earth-loving wife that I should fly. Speaking to Ruby's feelings of being trapped, I pointed out that the plane offered wings of freedom. "Honey, you wouldn't be trapped by dead-end roads, dark seashores and towering mountains." Admittedly, she struggled with these reasons, yet she also knew that more than any other people, Alaskans accepted air travel as a routine means of transportation. Still, I didn't mention the tundra decorated with planes or the tales of disappearances in the inlet and mountain alleyways—she was well aware of the risks.

I couldn't refute her logic about paying off medical school loans; regardless, in the spring of 1956, I bought a 1947 red, green, and silver J-3 Cub with a 75 hp engine and a controllable pitch wooden prop. The Christmas-tree-colored plane cost $1,500 with wheels and skis, and an additional $1,000 for floats.

Finding the right place to take flying lessons was not as easy as I'd anticipated. At the first place I inquired about lessons, I was told I would have to learn to fly wheels before floats. At the next place, Barton Air Service, I asked again if they taught initial flying on floats.

"Certainly," the young attendant answered. I signed up.

"Bring your plane to our dock at 5:00 p.m. tomorrow and you'll have your first lesson," the middle-aged, well-muscled instructor cordially told me.

Hesitantly I admitted, "I don't know anything about airplanes—I don't even know how to start mine, let alone taxi it to your dock." At that point, no one could have told me that someday I'd be taking off and landing on rivers, mud flats, or mountaintops.

For my first lesson, I walked along the docks on the shoreline and brought the instructor over to my plane. We began with the basics: starting the plane.

During the following weeks, I diligently studied my flight instruction book and nearly every evening and weekend headed over to Lake Hood. I'd splash through the water with my hipboots; hop onto a float; pump out the floats, checking them for leaks; hand-prop the plane; and taxi over to my instructor. Taxiing over was no longer a problem, nor was "braking" for the dock. After a few close calls of nearly smashing into the dock, I'd learned to plan ahead and cut the throttle in time.

Ruby and the children often accompanied me to the lake. At the young age of eight months, Mark loved the planes, and even his busy wiggles subsided when he watched the planes buzz on taking off and splash in landing. On warm evenings, or "hot" days of 60 degrees, Ruth and Naomi waded in the clear water with a sandy bottom, pulling apart water weeds that resembled bamboo fishing poles. "Fishing pole weeds" the girls called the 12- to 16-inch stalks which easily pulled apart into short segments.

One evening, as my instructor and I taxied from Lake Spenard toward the channel to Lake Hood, I saw a pair of floats bobbing on the waves at one end of the lake. "What are those floats doing over there?" I asked. "And why are they upside down?"

"There's a plane hanging under the water beneath those floats," my instructor calmly explained. "It belongs to a student of mine. Apparently she relaxed the stick upon landing and the plane flipped."

"Did she get out?"

"Oh yes, and I think she learned a lesson she'll never forget."

The chilling scene was still vivid in my mind as we docked at Barton's Air Service and my instructor climbed out of the plane. Before bounding off the floats and onto the dock, as he usually did, leaving me to taxi to my tiedowns, he casually said, "I'd like you to take the plane up by yourself."

"Solo? No! Not today." I silently shouted, remembering the plane beneath the water and looking up to a gray, formidable sky.

Sensing my reluctance, he assured me, "You'll do fine." And then he turned and walked away.

Slowly, I taxied back through the channel to Lake Spenard for takeoff. Even though I knew the seat behind me where my instructor sat was empty, I found myself talking out loud as I went down my checklist: fuel, oil pressure, magnetos. The instructions were clearly impressed on my mind.

Takeoff was not the difficult part, although a floatplane takeoff requires a different technique than a wheel takeoff. I gave the plane full throttle and pulled back slightly on the stick until after a few seconds of acceleration, the floats partially lifted out of the water. I could feel them teetering on the surface and eased forward on the stick, allowing the floats to plane out on top of the water like a water ski. Because of their hydrodynamic design, there was now the least amount of drag in the water, and the plane could more easily lift out of the water. This "getting on the step" felt familiar.

The blustery weather actually worked for me, as the rough water prevented the floats from forming a suction on the water's surface. On glassy water, I'd learned to tilt the wings slightly and lift one float off the water at a time, breaking the suction and allowing freedom for takeoff.

With waves of apprehension, I climbed out over the lake, almost immediately encountering light rain and chop. As I turned to a downwind pattern, visibility rapidly deteriorated as the rain increased. The plane seemed so small and fragile. I was scared! How had I gotten myself into this? My first flight in a barnstorming plane at age 15 over the suntanned Kansas wheatfields had been fun—like I thought learning to fly would be—not death-inviting like this!

As I turned to the crosswind leg, I peered through my rain-splattered windshield, searching for the green light from the tower. Only about 10 percent of the planes had radios, so most of our control was by flashing red or green lights. The controllers in the tower so precisely flashed the lights at the particular aircraft that the solid light chased away any doubts as to the intended message and intended receiver.

At last the tower flashed the welcoming green light and I cautiously made my approach.

Just as in takeoff, the water's surface again advised me. At least I didn't have to worry about a mirror-clear lake and lack of depth perception. The stormy waves actually made judging distance easier.

I glanced over to the shoreline for further reference. Searching for the water's surface, I let the plane settle with its nose up. Even stalling a few feet off the surface would jolt the pilot since shocks didn't accompany the floats.

To my relief, the floats flawlessly skimmed over the lake. Then, remembering my fellow student's fate, I kept the stick buried in my stomach until I came off the step and the floats settled into the water. I wiped my damp forehead as I taxied back to my instructor.

"Fine job. I knew you could do it!" my instructor slapped me on the back. "You may practice solo from now on."

"Not today, thanks," I sighed.

As I taxied back to my tie-downs, I thought to myself, "Only two weeks ago, I couldn't even start this plane. Now I just tookoff and landed by myself." I couldn't believe it.

Four weeks later and with 40 more hours I went for my ticket, passing the exam with 100 percent.

Little did I know that my soloing experience of soupy

weather, fast prayer, trepidation, dry mouth, and damp forehead would typify many of my flying experiences to come, and that someday I would be a real bush pilot with over 3,000 hours. All I knew was that I'd made it: "Flying or Bust!"

Now what was that Wally had said about hunting with the J-3?

4
The Thanksgiving Day moose
November 1956—January 1957

"Well, Paul, what do you say we try a moose hunt?" I asked my good friend Paul Carlson as we sat in our living room amidst the cacaphony of children playing after supper.

Just days before, earlier in November, I'd received my land rating with my J-3, so not only could I land with floats, but with wheels and skis as well. Alaska was one big landing strip of lakes in the summer for a floatplane. In snow-covered winter Alaska, I saw skis as my ticket to landing nearly anywhere; thus, I purchased a set of wooden skis.

Paul and I spent a lot of time together. To begin with, Ruby and I had heeded the suggestion of the Welcome Wagon greeter and turned to a church to establish relationships. In the case of Paul and his wife, Irene, our friendship had gone a step further, and we moved from our house on Lake Otis Road into Paul and Irene's house on Oak Street. This unusual arrangement was the result of the Carlson's financial debt from Paul's previous work in logging and trucking. I also was paying off my debt from medical school, so the arrangement met both needs.

Paul now worked in a grocery store and supplemented our food budget with broken packages of macaroni, rice, flour, sugar, and cake mixes. Irene, a home economics teacher, taught classes at the Community College and at the Elmendorf Air Force Base grade school. Their daughter, Nancy, attended college "Outside" in Minnesota. They turned their one-car garage into a bedroom and moved into that, graciously inviting our family to use the two bedrooms of the small house. In commune style, Paul, Irene, and our family shared the one bathroom, closet-sized kitchen, hallway dining room, and crowded living room.

As we visited this evening, Naomi and Ruth mooed and snorted with their toy farm animals fenced in beneath the dining room table. Apparently they still had some memory of their Kansas farmland roots. Mark, our future musician, played a mere 10 seconds of each record side on his record player before flipping it over. Behind this noise, dishes clattered as Ruby and Irene cleaned up the kitchen.

"Ok, Doc. I've been up with you a few times around Anchorage, and I think I'm brave enough to try a hunt," replied Paul, with the ever-present twinkle in his eye.

Paul spent his youth in Minnesota. Neither of us had ever hunted anything larger than a midwest coyote or jackrabbit. Paul had a 30.06. I bought a 300 H & H. After several sessions of going to target practice and listening to solicited and unsolicited hunting advice, we planned our moose hunt. As was to become my pattern, my initial hunting preparation was well thought-out.

We acquainted ourselves with hunting regulations and studied the maps of various hunting areas. Finally, on Thanksgiving Day, we took off from the snow-packed surface of Lake Hood in the crisp zero sunrise. I knew one rule of small plane flying was to cross a body of water at its narrowest point and to gain a safety margin of altitude in case of engine failure. I figured that at 2,000 feet I could glide across the Cook Inlet if an emergency arose, so I climbed to that altitude before heading south across the inlet to the Kenai Peninsula.

The northern half of the Kenai Peninsula resembled Minnesota, with a myriad of lakes surrounded by spruce trees. Most of the foot-thick ice on these lakes was covered with a six-inch layer of puffy snow. Seasoned Alaska hunters assured us that the moose would be on the lakes, so we dropped down to a few hundred feet to see for ourselves. Sure enough, on the second lake, we spotted three large moose—although we weren't sure about our judgment of what constituted "small" or "large." In any case, these critters were obviously much bigger than my dairy cows.

"Paul, this is going to be easier then I expected," I said as I cut the throttle to silently drift down on the lake in anticipation of a feather-light landing in front of the moose.

"Yes, our Thanksgiving moose is just waiting for us," he replied with boyish enthusiasm.

The landing was feather light, but much to our chagrin the moose were gone. They had fled into the woods. We were puzzled. Then we surmised the obvious; moose were wild game, unlike cattle, and would have to be stalked. We took off with a cloud of snow bursting behind us and resumed our search for other moose.

After a half hour, we spotted a lone bull on the edge of a small lake. With Moose Hunting Lesson #1 firmly in my mind, I decided to land on an adjacent lake and stalk the moose through the woods.

This lake did not resemble the one I'd previously landed on. Unlike the first snow-cushioned lake, which had been protected from the wind, this black-streaked lake was windblown with glare ice. I pushed aside the questions in my mind about its differentness.

As an innocent, inexperienced new ski pilot, I landed as usual. Even with the propeller completely stopped in front of us, the plane hurtled across the lake. There was no snowy resistance or drag to stop us, and the trees at the edge of the lake loomed taller and taller.

We both sat speechless in our seats, comprehending the danger, yet not really believing this was happening. My mind raced around trying to remember formal flying instructions or informal hangar talk. Desperately, I turned the plane sideways, hoping to develop more ski friction. No such luck.

"Hang on!" I yelled, as we hit the slightly inclined shoreline. I fully expected us to nose over, but instead we bounced to a stop with only one wingtip nudging the brush next to the trees.

We sat listening to our heartbeats. Then as I handed Paul his gun and followed him out the door into the silent whiteness, I asked, "Are you still brave enough to fly with me?"

"Well, we made it, didn't we?" he said grinning quickly, then crunching away on the hard-packed snowy shoreline toward the other lake—and the Thanksgiving moose. In a short time, we emerged on the other side of the snow-hushed woods, expecting to see our moose waiting for us. No moose. No sound. No movement. Then as we were about to go back, I caught a slight movement out of the corner of my eye, and saw, rather than heard, our intended prize running through the woods. It was an incredible sight to see the half-ton, full-racked animal lumbering through the dense forest with nary a sound.

Sensing danger, the enormous animal stopped broadside at 200 yards, looking at us with his colossal nose, gigantic ears, and beady eyes. His instinctive hesitation gave us the edge, and at 150 yards, I aimed and fired—one shot. Much to my astonishment, the moose dropped on the spot.

"Do you think he's really dead?" I asked Paul in disbelief.

"There's only one way to find out," said Paul.

We ran through the ankle-deep snow, around stumps and windfall, and over the uneven snowy ground toward the moose, then stopped a short distance away, not wanting the beast to terrify us by an unexpected resurrection. We edged closer and poked the moose with our guns. He remained motionless.

"We did it!" we hollered in unison, slapping each other on the back.

Then, with sobering reality, we stared at each other. "What do we do now?" was reflected on both our faces.

"It must be like butchering a corn-fed steer," I suggested, as I pulled out my hunting knife to cut its throat and drain the blood. I studied the moose at my feet. He must have weighed at least 1,000 pounds. I looked up around me, for some reason expecting to see a barn rafter with block and tackle, or winch, with which to hang the moose. "This isn't Kansas, Toto," I mumbled under my breath, realizing we didn't even have a rope, much less these other conveniences.

We managed to bleed the moose, then farmerlike went about the business of gutting and skinning the monster. I felt as though I was working with a plastic knife as we struggled with the tough hide.

Later I learned that, unlike farmers working with beef, which required skinning and which enjoyed the sanitary conditions of hanging in a barn, hunters would quarter the meat, leaving the hide on to protect it when it was either dragged out or packed out, meat-side up.

"Hey, Doc," Paul commented when our monumental task was nearly complete. "The clouds have moved in. We'd better get back to Anchorage since we don't have a tent for night."

A few snowflakes hit my face as I mentally added "tent" beneath "rope" on my list of things to bring along next time. Maybe a sleeping bag would come in handy, too, just in case.

"By the way, how are we going to get all this meat in the plane?" asked Paul.

As I considered that dilemma, the monster moose seemed to be like a fishing story—growing in size.

"Maybe we should take out a hind quarter now, cover the rest with the hide, and come back another time," I suggested. I knew bear were in hibernation and wolves usually wouldn't eat meat handled by men. Paul agreed to leaving it in this outdoor icebox, so huffing and puffing we wrestled the remaining moose into a natural hollow and wrapped the hide around the meat mountain.

By the time I packed out the quarter and loaded the plane, the sky was heavy. Unlike landing, takeoff on the glare ice was relatively easy.

Nothing that followed was easy, though. Nearing the 15-mile stretch of Cook Inlet, I wondered if our hunting adventure was going to have a "happily ever after" conclusion. The barrier between us and our destination increased. As we crossed the inlet, lowering clouds pressed us toward the beckoning murky water. A strong headwind pushed us away from the Anchorage shoreline. Darkness shrouded Anchorage, allowing only patches of landmark lights to blink through. Added to all these treacherous conditions was our heavily loaded plane. My diagnosis of these facts was that the 2,000-foot altitude was no longer an adequate safety margin.

About halfway across the inlet, I remembered the gas gauge. The J-3 was an unsophisticated aircraft, with a simple gas gauge: a bobbing cork. The bobbing cork within the 13-gallon nose gas tank was attached to a wire, which poked outside the nose of the plane, near the windshield. A short wire meant "Find gas now!" since after the wire stopped bouncing, there was usually only 20 minutes of fuel left. As the wind buffeted the plane in the inky sky, I pulled out my flashlight to inspect the bobber. It wasn't floating.

Sucking in my breath sharply, I turned around to Paul in the back seat. "We'd better do some praying. I'm prepared to meet my Maker, but I'm not ready for a cold, wet grave."

It seemed like an eternity as we fought our way to the Anchorage shore; and even then, we weren't home free. The Lake Hood tower was closed. As we wandered through the darkness, knowing the engine could sputter to a stop at any time, we located the few channel marker lights between Lake Hood and Lake Spenard. The J-3 had no landing lights, and I hoped and prayed that there were no other planes in my pathway. Slowly I eased into the blackness between the dim markers. The skis reached down and with a bounce found the hard-packed snow. Very slowly we felt our way along as we taxied to our tiedowns. I knew we'd been flying on fumes and prayer, but not until I shut down the throttle did the plane engine stop.

We sat in tired silence, feeling our shoulders untense, and thanking the Lord for safety. It had been a long day.

The solid ground beneath our feet felt great as we unloaded the plane and headed home. By the time we walked through the door, Paul's eyes were twinkling again.

Over the next month, we nearly wore out the first half of our hunting story, recounting the adventure to anybody who would listen. Finally, I embarked on the last half of the story. This time, I wrote down the tale and shared it with my parents in Reedley, California, and their local paper, the Reedley Exponent, published it. The story went like this:

"Last Saturday Paul and I planned to fly out to get the rest of our moose, which was across the inlet and about 50 miles away from here. I loaded the plane with tools to get the moose out and waited for Paul to return from work, but since he didn't come by 10 A.M., I took off alone.

About 30 miles out, ice fog began closing in from the Cook Inlet. I stayed on the edge of the fog and landed on the lake where we had left the moose. I found the moose frozen solid and in good condition. For the next several hours, I chopped and sawed apart the three remaining quarters and backpacked them to the plane. Even though my task was accomplished, I could not take off since fog had closed in around the lake within an hour after I landed.

Freezing rain then started and soon the plane was iced over. I tried once to get off the lake, but fog surrounded the entire area. Knowing I was grounded for the night, I found some dry wood, built a good fire, and tried to stay dry. I put my sleeping bag over my snowshoes and tried to sleep under the wings of the plane. It got dark at 4 P.M., so it was a long night.

The next day was just as foggy as the day before, but on my third attempt to fly out I managed to fly between fog layers over to the inlet, but I could not get across. From my low altitude, I looked for lakes with tents or cabins for shelter. After awhile, I found a rundown cabin beside a large lake and landed. Blinding snow covered the plane as I cut the engine. The cabin proved to be a God-send because it was still warm— the stove had been used only a few hours previously. I spent Sunday night alone in this warm cabin.

Monday morning at 9:30 A.M., I saw an Air Force rescue plane, a two-motored Albatross, looking for me. I had filed a flight plan and was overdue since 3 P.M. Saturday. When they spotted my plane, they dropped messages to me in a bright orange bag. They had looked for me Sunday, but couldn't see through the fog. They said the Anchorage airport was completely closed in with fog. Since I was o.k., I didn't request help. Knowing they would notify Ruby that I was all right, I could rest at ease and wait for a clearing.

Monday afternoon, an Indian trapper happened to come by the cabin, and he turned out to be one of my patients from last November. He made us pancakes and fried beaver meat. We had a good time talking about hunting, his family, and his first visit to Anchorage. He had a short wave radio so we kept in touch with Anchorage weather.

On Tuesday, the ice fog was still hanging low and the temperature remained near zero. Finally at 1:50 P.M. the Civil Air Administration (CAA) weather report stated that Anchorage airport was open, so I made my sixth attempt to come in.

The fog was down to 1,300 feet over the inlet, with large ground fog patches near Anchorage, but I made it down with no problem just before dark. I had 15 minutes of fuel left when I landed.

Later I found out that a bush pilot and our church pastor had tried to come across the inlet to find me about 30 minutes before I came in, but they were forced back by fog below 500 feet, so I certainly felt God had opened the Inlet for a short time for me. I was fortunate to come through when I did because we had heavy ice fog the next three days.

I never realized I had so many friends until I came back. Church, hospital personnel, and even patients showed a great concern over my safety. While I was stuck across the inlet, some of the church women stayed with Ruby to help pass the time. After the Air Force plane made contact with me, they notified her of my safety.

Last night we thawed out a front quarter of moose and cut and wrapped it. We're having a big moose meat supper this coming Friday evening with two medical families."

And so, the second half of the Thanksgiving Day Moose story did have a happy ending as the "hunters lived happily ever after." At least one hunter was wiser and bought two down-filled army sleeping bags, which were good for -40 to -50 F—for who knew what lay ahead?

5
Lime Village evacuation
January 1957

Snuggled between the white blanket of clouds above and the bed of snow beneath us, we flew above Stony River searching for Lime Village. Mike, the pilot of the Cessna 180, maintained an altitude of 2,000 feet while looking out his side window into the afternoon overcast. I rubbed my army green wool mitten against my window and tried to detect any distinguishing marks against the nearly totally black and white environment. Nothing but sameness.

This reminded me of my trip to Noatak with Tommy, where the whiteness spread like a never-ending roll of tissue paper in front of us. There was one difference, however: Tommy was an experienced bush pilot, familiar with the country and his desti-

Lime Village evacuation 33

nation, whereas neither Mike nor I had much experience in bush flying or in this hide-and-go-seek winter village-finding.

As my eyes continued to scan the riverbank, my thoughts drifted back to early that morning when I'd walked into the hospital, expecting a routine day. I remembered the question aimed at me by the hospital medical director before I could even take off my coat: "Didn't you volunteer to fly out for all medical emergencies?" And I remembered my quick-fire, "Sure! Where's the emergency?"

Now as the riverbank became a repeating pattern of white snow and black-green spruce trees, and the gas indicator subtracted the green area and moved toward the red, and the minutes added up into another half hour, I asked the same question: "Where's the emergency?"

The urgent emergency message had come that morning via radio through the Sparrevohn Air Force Base, which was located across the Cook Inlet and through the Alaska Mountain Range:

"A baby is very ill in Lime Village and will probably need to be evacuated. The villagers will mark off an area on the river near the village where you can land. Come quickly."

At this moment, Mike and I were searching for that small Indian village with marked-off landing area.

I'd found Mike at Merrill Field where I checked for a charter plane. He was a low-time pilot but his Cessna had a wheel-ski combination. In fact, his plane was more equipped for the bush landing than he was. Still, I was confident that even with our combined lack of experience, our combined optimism would get us to our destination. It wasn't until here, 200 miles west of Anchorage, following Stony River and without a hint of civilization, that I realized we were truly the blind leading the blind.

Together we'd studied the areonautical charts to locate Lime Village. One chart we looked at had a village called "Hungry" marked where Lime Village should have been. Later I learned that someone had jokingly called the village "Hungry" and the name stuck.

We traced our route from Anchorage, west through Merrill Pass in the Alaskan Mountain Range, to Stony River. We would follow Stony River to Lime Village, in the Lime Hills.

"I'm sure we should have been there by now," I finally said. "Let's turn around, drop down to 500 feet, and backtrack."

About ten minutes later, I suddenly recognized smoke spiraling upward from what appeared to be a mound of rock. We circled low and immediately people popped out from the now-discernible dozen cabins. Children waved, women pointed upriver toward the east, while men hitched up their dog teams. We banked the plane, and about a mile upriver we discovered spruce branches marking out our runway. Mike made several low passes. "What do you think, Doc?" he asked.

"It looks o.k. to me," I calmly replied, in spite of my apprehension as I realized he'd never landed on anything like this before. "Let's give it a try." I checked my seatbelt, hooked my hands around the metal bars running beneath the seat, and looked out the window and down at the skis to be sure he'd pulled the wheels out of position.

Mike pulled full flaps as we flared down for a ski landing. So far so good. I thought we'd made it until the rough ice hit the skis like a sledge hammer, violently throwing us around in our seats and sounding like a jackhammar. The plane skidded and clattered around on the airstrip, until eventually it slid against a short pressure ridge and stopped.

We looked at each other in amazement. "Doc, do you still have your teeth?" Mike asked, after he turned off the engine. Looking outside, he added, "I'll never let anyone choose my landing spot again."

"Things certainly aren't the same on the ground as they look from the air," I said, shaking my head.

We got out of the plane and checked the skis. "We're lucky these skis didn't tear apart," Mike said. Just as we finished pulling the cowling cover over the engine to keep it warm, a group of dogsleds arrived. I'd seen the dog races at the Fur Rendezvous, but this was my first time to see *real* dog teams up close. The dogs looked quite thin. Actually, their masters, who greeted us with friendly smiles, were none too heavy either. I wondered if this had anything to do with why the village was nicknamed "Hungry."

Mike and I were each invited to get on different sleds. "This will be great!" I thought to myself as I climbed in. I imagined smoothly gliding along, just as I'd seen the dogsleds do in front of our house. Just think, I could go back home and tell my family and friends that I'd actually ridden in a dog sled.

The dogteam driver yelled at the dogs to "Mush," gave the

sled a push, and ran behind while holding on until the sled picked up speed, and then he jumped onto the back runners. My enthusiasm waned as we bounced and careened between pressure ridges over the rough ice. It was a replay of our landing, except for one thing: the plane seats were cushioned whereas this hard seat had no shock absorber. After fifteen minutes, my misery ended and I gingerly extracted my aching body from the sled. So much for the glamour of dogsled riding.

"The baby is there," said Jacob, our designated host, pointing toward an older cabin a short distance away. Slowly, Mike and I followed him along a narrow snow path as some of the children tagged behind us, trying to hide behind one another and smiling shyly. When I smiled back, several giggled, bravely ran up and touched my arm, then ran back into the group.

Seeing the inside of an Indian cabin was another first for me. We kicked the snow off our boots then walked through the door, which was framed by icicles stretching from the roof nearly to the ground. A stuffy warm heat enveloped us as we looked around the dimly lit 20-by-24 foot log cabin. Besides the anemic January sun filtering through the overcast and passively standing outside the small smudged windows, the only light came from the kerosene lamp sitting on a wooden table amidst a jumble of powdered milk, green melmac dishes, a pocket knife, wood shavings, and a raw red fox hide.

A fat 50-gallon oil barrel stove produced the heavy heat in the room. The Natives took oil drums, turned them on their sides, set them on legs, cut a hole for a door at one end, and inserted a stove pipe at the other. They then attached a flat piece of metal on top of the round barrel side on which they could heat water.

On a bed in one corner sat a young Native woman nursing her baby. "Jean, this is Dr. Gaede," said Jacob.

"Doctor, my baby John has cold a long time," said Jean, as I sat down on a chair near her. "Now he coughing more and more. He has high fever. He don't eat good. He getting skinny." Her concern was evident as she continued. "He don't act right. Others in village cough much, too, but they not sick like my baby John."

I examined the frail baby, who had a feeble cry and a weak productive cough. He was pale, in spite of his Indian-brown skin, and I guessed he was anemic. He had a high fever, some evidence of dehydration, and moisture in both lungs. I mentally added up these symptoms.

"Jean, your baby is very sick and probably has pneumonia," I quietly told her. "I'll have to take him with me to the ANS hospital in Anchorage—or else. . . ."

"Doctor, you take him now," Jean quickly replied as though she had thought through the alternatives. Within minutes, she had gathered some clothes for him, wrapped several more blankets around him, and handed him to me. She walked us to the door, but before opening it, stopped me, pulled the worn flannel blanket away from baby John's face, and kissed him on the forehead.

I was not eager to take another dogsled ride, but with the fading winter afternoon daylight, I knew my only other option, walking back to the plane, would detain us from the necessary immediate takeoff.

When we got back to the strip, I handed the baby to Jacob while Mike and I walked around on the runway to determine the least perilous path for takeoff. We did a better job of estimating our takeoff course than we did with our landing, and soon we were heading back to Anchorage, completing our journey just as the sun fell out of sight, leaving a pink, deepening to purple afterglow against the Chugach Mountains.

When we landed, Mike and I congratulated ourselves on our bush-flying success, and I headed over to the hospital with baby John.

X-rays and a laboratory workup showed that the baby not only had pneumonia, but also active tuberculosis. He would have to stay in the hospital many months before returning home.

A medical survey in the early 1930s estimated that over one-third of Native deaths in Alaska were attributable to tuberculosis. In 1949 alone, 230 people died of tuberculosis in Alaska, this rate was 23 percent higher than that of the United States. A startling example of these statistics came from a schoolteacher in Barrow, who in 1946 reported that of thirty children who entered school between the ages of five and six, only six lived to finish. Following its introduction to Alaska in the eighteenth century, the scourge of tuberculosis was the most urgent and important health issue in Alaska.

Subsequently, less than two months later, the Anchorage

Lime Village evacuation 37

ANS hospital again received a similiar emergency radio call from Sparrevohn Air Force Base. Apparently, a dog team from Lime Village had arrived with another urgent plea for medical help. This time it was for a child, about two years old, who was very ill with possible pneumonia. Could medical help come as soon as possible?

"Elmer, are you game for another mercy flight?" my supervisor asked me.

"Sure," I replied. "I'll inquire about a charter plane." A pilot and plane were available the next day and even the weather was forecast to cooperate. This time I would fly into Sparrevohn, twenty miles south of Lime Village, rather than to Lime Village itself, and the sick child would come in on dogsled. I thought about my dog sled experience and felt sorry for the child already. Twenty miles by dogsled. Maybe the Natives were used to the bumping and jostling.

Sparrevohn was a restricted air force airfield, and authorization was required. We called ahead to request permission to land on the 3,700-foot runway.

This time, my pilot, Dennis, was an experienced bush pilot and already acquainted with flying through the mountains and landing at Sparrevohn. We fired up the plane at noon because the CAA weather report indicated earlier fog in the mountains and in low areas, which was to dissipate. Sparrevohn was giving out reports of sky obscured and less than a quarter-mile visibility, but this was expected to change by the time we got there.

The flight route again took us west, over the Cook Inlet. As we approached the Alaskan Mountain Range, wide bands of blue-gray clouds allowed only a partial view of Merrill Pass. These we skirted and then flew above the fog patches crouched in the Pass valley to Stony River. We then cut over to Cairn Mountain.

Although we had flown over only small patches of fog along our route, we were disappointed to find the entire valley at Sparrevohn socked in, with no visibility of the ground from the air.

The Sparrevohn fixed air force base radio operator informed us that the fog was rolling in and out so that occasionally the runway was visible.

"Go into a holding pattern to wait for a break in the fog," he suggested.

"We can try making a special VFR (Visual Flight Rules) approach," Dennis suggested. However, there would be only one attempt with no mistakes since the runway ended at the base of the 3,800-foot Cairn Mountain on the north. The runway was elevated on the north end; therefore, all landings were made to the north and all takeoffs to the south.

I had never landed in below-minimal VFR conditions. We circled about thirty minutes, after which Dennis turned to me and said, "Doc, my fuel is nearly half gone. If we can't find an opening in the fog soon, we're going back to Anchorage. I'll talk to the radio operator once more and ask about the thin spots."

Through the cloud base of 500 to 800 feet, we could intermittantly see patches of ground. "Hey, there's a hole!" exclaimed Dennis, just as he was reaching for his microphone to call the operator. "It's at the south end of the runway—just where we need it. Let's try it."

We slipped the plane, making a quick descent using opposite aileron (wing) and rudder (tail) control through the hole and pulled flaps, squeezing under the fog, where we could see nearly all the runway. I was still trying to get used to the dropping feeling this caused, especially as a passenger, rather than a pilot. Since we were below normal approach pattern, we skimmed the terrain, and dropped in on the numbers on the runway.

As we touched down, we rolled past a wrecked military cargo plane to my right. Yes, this was a another hazardous landing. Were there such things as "normal" bush landings, I wondered?

An air force officer met us and took us to a nearby barrack. There we found not only one sick child from Lime Village, but two—both boys between the ages of two and three. They cooperated with my examination. Neither smiled nor giggled as had the other children I'd met at Lime Village, but instead were coughing, feverish, and listless, and obviously had pneumonia.

"Men, it looks as though you're right," I said, turning to the two dogsled drivers. "These children are very sick and I'll need to take them both back to Anchorage ANS hospital."

The men nodded in agreement and then handed me the bags with the children's clothing. "We were afraid our babies would die. Go now." The men solemnly patted the two childrens' heads and walked out the door. The children, faces flushed with fever, expressed no anxiety, but held on to each other's hands. Dennis walked out the door after them and looked up at the sky. "There are a few good holes up there, but let's get out now before any more trouble rolls in."

Complacently, the boys crawled into the back seat of the plane. Unlike healthy children, who would be intrigued by the new experience, they curled against each other and fell asleep even before we taxied up to the north end of the runway.

Taking off downhill was simple, and we easily climbed through the patchy fog. We leveled out at 6,000 feet and followed our same route back, pushing through the gray passes. As we emerged from our foggy tunnel, the bright sunlight greeted us, turning the mud flats silver and waking the children, who peered out the windows in amazement at the large city below.

Complete physical examinations with X-rays and laboratory tests revealed active tuberculosis and pneumonia in both children. These children would eventually recover, as would baby John, but the discovery of three children in the same village with active tuberculosis caused us great concern.

The following summer, a tuberculosis survey team was flown to Lime Village. The nurses and laboratory technicians carried with them a portable X-ray machine. The findings shocked us. Twenty-eight of the twenty-nine Natives had active tuberculosis. Lime Village was literally wiped out as all those with active tuberculosis had to leave the village for prolonged treatment. Needless to say, our 400-bed hospital soon reached capacity, with not only these villagers, but others, and we had to send many Native tuberculosis patients "outside" to the United States for treatment.

Later, when the Lime Village natives could return home, many chose to make a new start and relocate at Stony River Village along the Kuskokwim River.

Baby John had been just the tip of the iceberg in the unfolding saga of one village's encounter with the scourge of tuberculosis.

Notes

1. *Alaska Native Medical Center: A History, 1953–1983*, Robert Fortuine, Alaska Medical Center, 1986. p. 5.
2. Ibid., p. 6.
3. Ibid., p. 5.
4. Ibid., p. 6.

6
Out to get a bear rug
March 1956

We'd heard of him, the Brown Bear who stalked hunters. Just last year, a lone hunter tracked him, but never returned with a story much less a rug, and no one ever found him. I'd patched together the mangled bodies of men in the emergency room who had encountered similar killers.

Brown bear were a favorite topic with most hunters, hikers, and fishermen. The brown bear closely resembles its relative, the black bear, except that it is larger and has a more prominent shoulder hump. Color in itself is not reliable since both the brown and black bear come in varying shades of black-brown.

Some hunters sought out bear trophies in fall, before the

bears entered dormancy in November. Jim and I, however, decided to wait until spring. Jim, an employee at Elmendorf Air Force Base, lived next door to us. On many occasions, he told hunting stories, which kindled my interest and carried me into my first hunting experiences.

I was a naive *cheechako* ("tenderfoot"), and a novice pilot—a prime candidate for trouble. My ambitions, nonetheless, equaled those of gold-seeking hopefuls compelled to take advantage of this rich territory and make their wildest dreams come true.

Now, returning to the Talkeetna Mountains on my fourth bear hunt of the season, I thought back to several weeks ago when Jim and I were up in my J-3, winding in and out through several valleys. Suddenly we'd caught sight of distinct, fresh bear tracks, black against the white ridge.

Unlike moose tracks, which followed a gradual ascent along the mountainside, these tracks shot in a straight line, up one ridge and down the other. As we followed the tracks, we noticed that the bear actually slid down the ridges as though they were great playground slipper slides.

After a short distance, the tracks strayed away from the mountains to the open country, where only an occassional bush pierced the unmarred snow. We looked ahead, certain we would easily find him in this unprotected area.

Then we spotted him, at first only a brownish-black object at the end of the trail. Spiraling closer, we dropped to less than 100 feet above the moving mass, making several passes. At every pass he tried first to hide, then finding no seclusion, jumped toward us in challenge. Standing nearly 9 feet tall on his hind feet, he clawed at the air beneath us, his mouth open in rage.

Here he was, the Alaskan brown bear and the largest meat-eating animal that lives on land. He reminded me of a 1,200- to 1,400-pound Kansas bull, which was possible, since brownies can weigh over 1,500 pounds.

In the northland, every sportsman yearns to have a bear rug trophy. "This bear obviously does not aspire for the glories of the hearthside," I shouted to Jim above the engine's roar.

"No, but I think he's in for a surprise," he confidently yelled back. "Let's put this thing down and get what we came for."

All this transpired on March 30 and marked my introduction to bear hunting. At 6:00 A.M., with a 30° F temperature, Jim and had loaded my ice-glazed J-3 on skis at Lake Hood. Yes, I was an amateur and minimized the lift-reducing effects that frost, much less ice, had on a plane. Fortunately, however, even with Jim's 200 pounds, the plane leaped off the ice-covered lake. The higher altitude, rising sun, and wind melted the plane ice as we headed north over a narrow finger of Cook Inlet and toward the Talkeetna Mountains.

Before us, Mt. McKinley and Mt. Foraker stood as glittering landmarks in the clear horizon, their peaks haloed by clouds. I'd carefully planned this trip step by step and filed a flight plan, which took us first to Willow, 40 miles from Anchorage. There we followed the Alaska Railroad for 40 miles to Talkeetna, at the base of the Alaskan and Talkeena mountain ranges. Appropriately named by the Indians, "where the rivers meet," the small one-street town with miscellaneous log cabins and roadhouses was located at the confluence of the Susitna, Talkeetna, and Chulitna rivers.

We flew east, into the Talkeetna Mountains, to a ridge where Jim had successfully spotted brown bear on previous years. Skirting the ridges at 3,000 feet, we saw moose, but no sign of bear. Only the dark shadow of the plane flitted against the still background.

"Doc, I think we're a few weeks early," said Jim.

"Let's try it to the west," I suggested, not ready to admit defeat so quickly on my first bear hunt.

I looked out the front window at my "gas gauge" wire. We decided to stop at Talkeetna to refuel and revise our flight plan. Soon afterward, we flew west in the clear, dark blue sky toward Mt. Yenlo in the Alaskan Range.

It was then, after canvassing the valleys and ridges that we saw him. In full fury he pawed the air. The killer brownie was there for us—if we could get to him. Over a small hill, I spotted a flat, smooth, potential landing area about two blocks square and only three blocks from the bear. We made several more passes over the bear, attempting to nag him closer to our landing spot.

"Keep your eye on him!" I said to Jim. "I'm going to land."

As soon as we touched the unbroken white carpet, I felt a tremendous drag. I was in trouble. In my assessment for a landing strip, I'd checked for smoothness, not snow condition. Immediately, I applied full throttle, attempting to free myself from the clinging snow and takeoff again. Regardless of my efforts, we gradually lost speed and even with the engine protesting, the plane wallowed to a stop. My hopes sank, as did the tail, which settled into the deep snow.

Later I learned that, before commiting oneself to landing, it was wise to first do a touch-and-go, where the plane skis would just skim the snow's surface, testing the softness and depth, without landing.

Ignorantly, I assured Jim that we could worry about takeoff later, after we got the bear. I foolishly failed to consider the chances of the killer brownie turning on us. In this open valley with only sporadic clumps of trees, where could we find safety? A retreat to our plane with its thin fabric would only tease the short-tempered bear, who with a single swat of a front paw could kill a caribou or moose.

In spite of these facts, we fastened on our bear-paw snowshoes and checked our weapons. We were positive that between us and danger stood Jim's 300 Magnum, and my 30.06 rifle and .357 Magnum revolver.

Walking on snowshoes demanded concentration. Practicing in the gravel pit across from our house, I'd quickly learned the consequences of not keeping the toes up. All too often, I'd toed down, catching a tip in the snow and plunging head first into the snow. Or I'd walk with my legs too close together, the insides of the snowshoes stepping on top of one another, then dipping toward the center and causing my knees to knock together.

I set out after Jim, my more experienced friend. Somewhere before us was a killer bear, and behind us trailed my messy snowshoe path to my plane which was stuck in the snow. The scene was something that could have come out of a Laurel and Hardy movie. In this precarious condition, we approached the area where we had last seen the bear.

Fortunately, we were downwind. Jim scrunched down and then poked his head over the crest. Standing up for a moment and looking all around, he called over his shoulder, "He's gone, but boy what a trail he left for us."

Twelve-inch paw tracks four feet apart in the deep snow showed us the bear's haste in getting away and left us a definitely marked trail. Through our rifle scopes, we followed his trail for about a half mile toward the mountains, hoping to find him in our sights. No such luck.

Trudging after our trophy, we soon removed our coats as we

sweated from the exertion and the sunshine reflecting off the snow. Within a half hour our efforts were rewarded as we noticed a dark spot against the glaring whiteness. Even with the rifle scope, this appeared to be only a black ball. Drawing closer, we finally saw the outline of a brownie. Jim advised me to stay by a grove of trees and that we should try our shots with a solid gun support.

The bear, uphill and sitting down appeared to be about 400 yards away. We balanced our rifles in limbs of the trees, placed the scope cross hair right below the bear's shoulders, and began shooting. One. Two. Three . . . Six. The bear casually turned to look at us. After a few more shots, he growled in annoyance, turned, and resumed his journey up the mountain. As he reached the ridge, we threw more lead at him.

We hustled up the hill after him and examined the spot where we had disturbed his sunning. There we saw that nearly all our shots had not even tickled his toes—but had only disturbed the snow a few feet below him. We'd misjudged the distance by 200 yards. At 600 yards, the drop of our bullets was more than we'd expected.

By now, the arduous trek had caught up with our enthusiasm. "I'll turn back now," I told Jim. "Let's go see what we can do about the plane."

Our exercise continued as we sweated and tramped out a 600-foot-long by 12-foot-wide runway with our snowshoes. Once we'd dug out the plane and placed the tail on solidly packed snow, the plane was easy to push around, and we used it to futher compact the makeshift runway.

Only one problem remained: a ravine abruptly ended the runway. "Jim, tell me immediately when we are airborne, otherwise I'll need to chop the throttle at the end of the runway." We both had our work cut out for us.

Giving the plane full power, I began gliding across the packed snow. I coaxed the tail off the runway. The airspeed indicator hesitantly edged upwards as we neared the end of the runway. Slowly I pulled the stick back at 45 mph and we said goodbye to the field.

"Doc, you only had inches to spare," said Jim, letting out his breath.

We easily tracked our brownie by air. His trail ambled across two valleys and returned to the ridge where we had seen his original tracks. Apparently his den was nearby.

Tired, sunburned, yet still excited, we landed on the late afternoon slush of Lake Hood. Already we were planning our next hunt.

Hunts two and three proved unsuccessful. Today was number four—and to be our last attempt this season to bring home Brown Beauty. With the middle of April "breakup," Lake Hood would soon become too dangerous for takeoff. This was our last chance.

Alaskans did not refer to "springtime," instead it was "breakup," signifying the time of year when river and lake ice brokeup and when the snow melted, forming its own lakes above the still frozen ground.

Just that morning, we'd discovered my plane in a foot of water as we arrived at 5:00 A.M. Undaunted, we had pulled the plane up onto the solid ice and had taken off.

Like a homing pigeon, the plane easily flew back to the Talkeetna Mountains. The previous week we'd spotted four bear dens in the area.

"It's about time these bear woke up," I impatiently said to Jim, as we flew low over the ridges, hoping the roar of the engine might serve as an alarm clock. At the same time I wanted to keep my distance. The previous year, two hunters were killed trying to lure a grizzly from his home. It was better to allow bear a voluntary debut.

"Look over there! There are tracks by that den," replied Jim.

The tracks only circled the immediate area.

"Maybe the morning air is too chilly for the Sleeping Beauties to take a morning walk," I commented.

We mentally marked these dens, then flew farther into the Talkeetna Range, exploring the hills and valleys and surveying six dens with evidence of activity.

"That gas bobber is kind of short," said Jim after awhile. "Let's go back to Talkeetna village, fuel up, and grab some lunch."

I glanced over at the fuel gauge. "We're o.k. yet," I said. "Let's just check once more to see if our trophy rugs are over at the first dens we spotted."

We flew back high over the ridges, when suddenly I shouted to Jim. "Look ahead! See the two brown bear!" Two golden bear romped in their front yard, about one-third of the way up a 2,400-foot mountain. They batted at one another, rolling and tumbling in play. Chasing one another, they would slide on their backs partway down the mountainside and then colliding against each other race back up to the top. Their play belied their dangerous natures.

"O.k., let's find a place to land—one we don't have to dig out of," urged Jim.

The ridge had several large, smooth snowfields. I put the plane down on a white bed about half a mile from our target. No problems this time.

Once again, we strapped on our snowshoes and made waffled tracks to a ridge overhanging our quarry. The wind was in our favor. We stopped and listened. The air was deathly silent. Did something know something we didn't? Were there eyes watching us? Slowly we peered over the loose, snowy ledge.

The bear playground, 200 yards below us, was empty. "Maybe the sunbathers had their quota of sunshine and returned home for another nap," I whispered to Jim.

"I just hope they're not somewhere watching us and considering making us playmates," said Jim, clutching his rifle and then standing up and looking all around.

We sat down to await new developments. After 45 minutes, Jim could take it no longer. He restlessly walked over toward a short tree about 40 feet away. About 20 feet before the tree, he dropped his 300 Magnum and pulled out his hunting knife. Optimistically, he trimmed out a gunrest.

Meanwhile, I scanned the scene around and below me with binoculars, hoping I hadn't overlooked some important factor in our hunting setup—such as a bear hunting us.

Suddenly, the two overgrown teddy bears burst into view from behind a large pine tree near their den. "Jim, they're back!" I yelled as I slid next to a tree for my gun rest.

Jim dashed for his gun. The bear, hearing us, started their wild scramble for safety. Jim's trigger finger quickly found its position and placed a bullet in the larger bear's shoulder, causing it to turn its head and bite the wound. His next shoulder shot threw it off balance and it rolled into a canyon 200 feet below.

For a moment, my first shot slowed down the smaller bear, but it continued gaining speed as it started downhill. The second shot went wild. The third shot hit paydirt and the bear dropped in its tracks.

"We did it! We got our bear rug trophies!" we congratulated

each other as we hurried as fast as snowshoes can go down the hill.

Skinning out our prizes was tough work. Even though we'd failed to check their pelts for rubbed areas, their blond-tipped fur was even throughout. It took us nearly three hours to remove their hides, by which time we were fairly saturated with bear oil. From nose to tail, the larger bear measured 8 feet and the smaller one 6½ feet. Unlike moose or caribou, the bear meat was greasy and not something our wives would want in the kitchen.

Since we hadn't eaten for ten hours, we were so weak that it took us grueling hours to slowly pack our treasures up the mountain to the plane. By this time, the midafternoon sun had softened the snow's crust. Packing in two full bear hides with heads, plus 120 pounds of hunting gear and my hefty partner, grossed our weight to the limit—and increased the sag of the tail.

I walked the ridge and measured 300 feet of good takeoff space before there was a steep drop-off. "We may have to drop off over the edge if we can't get enough airspeed for takeoff." I told Jim.

"Sounds like a thriller," he replied.

With full power, the J-3 slowly picked up speed on the soggy snow. The 300 feet rapidly disappeared beneath us and we dropped off the precipice, hovering in the emptiness, then, like a roller coaster, swooping down 1,000 feet before gradually leveling off. After awhile, our pulses leveled off, too.

Back at Talkeetna, Don Sheldon approached us when we landed at the Don Sheldon airstrip. Already an Alaskan legend, he had perfected high-risk glacier landings and flew teams of scientists and climbers onto Mt. McKinley.

About 50 feet away, he commented amiably, "Smells like you boys got your bear."

"Yep. This time we didn't just exercise the wildlife." I said. "We got our bear rug trophies."

I flew back to Anchorage, smiling to myself as I mentally listed my accomplishments over the last two years.

—fly on floats, wheels, and skis
—take off on lakes and mountains
—shoot a moose
—shoot a bear

—escort a Eskimo baby to the interior of Alaska
—fly into an Indian village
—helping organize the ANS hospital

When I'd bumped on into dusty Anchorage, I didn't know what the future would hold, I only knew I had dreams of adventure. Instead of satiating my desire for adventure, all these accomplishments only served to whet my appetite, to stoke the Alaskan Fever. I felt warm and restless. What could I do next?

Dusty car and campsite.

Ship Creek - July, 1955.

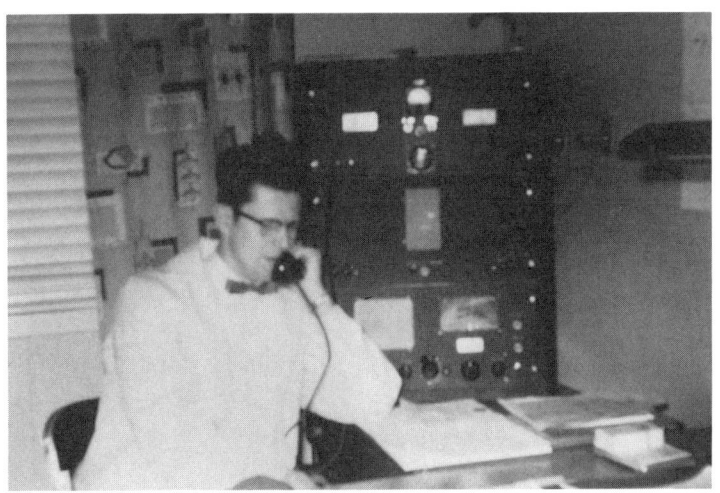

Radio schedule with the Villages - February, 1958.

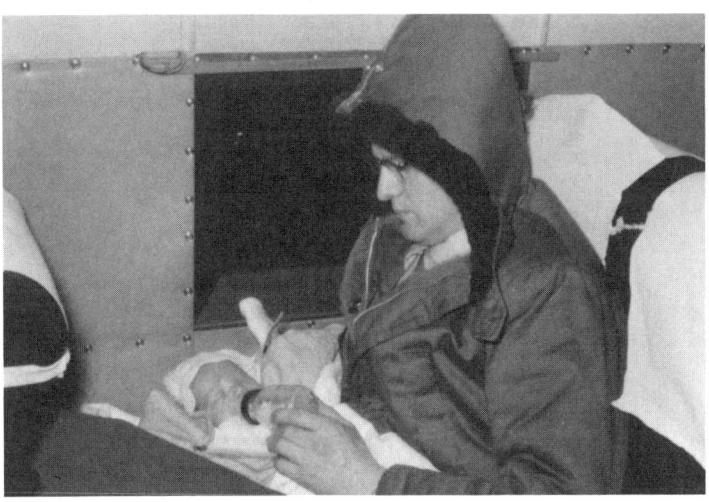

Feeding baby on plane trip to Kotzebue - January, 1956.

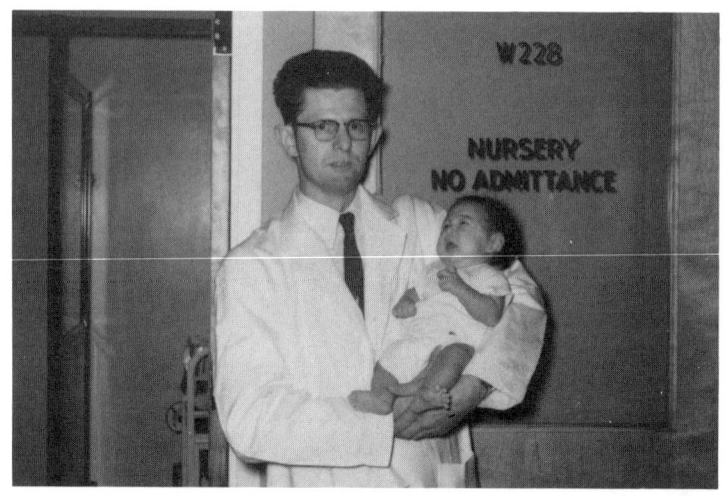

Elmer and baby ready for escort trip to Kotzebue - October, 1956.

Alaska Native Hospital - October, 1956.

Pediatric potty chair scene - November, 1956.

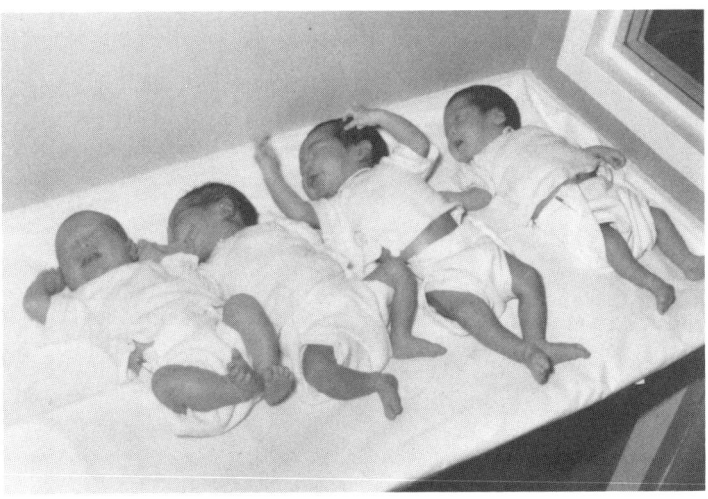

Three Eskimo newborn babies and Mark (their son) -
December, 1956.

My first moose - November, 1956.

Charlie's cabin at Manley Hot Springs.

Yukon Sternwheeler - July, 1958.

Our annual food supply.

Arriving at Kotzebue. Sled is our limousine - January, 1956.

Noorwik - landing on the river - March, 1958.

Anaktuvuk Pass - April, 1959.

Rambling Roy Groning - Tanana - Home of Reverend Roy Groning - March, 1957.

Missionary Navingers at Kaltag - April, 1959.

Hotel at Barrow - July, 1959.

Erosion in the lava on the floor of the Valley of Ten Thousand Smokes - June, 1957.

Our plane on the beach at Barrow - July, 1959.

Bringing our supplies to shore at Pt. Hope.

Me and the grizzly cub - April, 1957.

7
Assignment: Tanana
1957

I smelled it before I saw it. Smoke. I was flying cross-country from Anchorage to Tanana. Situated 300 miles north of Anchorage and 150 miles west of Fairbanks, Tanana stretched along the riverbank where the silty Tanana River lost itself in the mighty Yukon. This Athabascan Indian village was accessible only by plane or boat.

The smoke problem wasn't my first roadblock—or airblock—on this venture. The day before, on a bright blue July afternoon, I'd eagerly skimmed off Lake Hood and headed north, only to find puffy white thunderclouds brewing among the mountain peaks and spilling down into the valleys, blocking my route through Summit and toward Mt McKlinley Park.

What had prompted me to leave the familarities of Anchorage and head alone into the Interior, much more with my J-3, which was minimally equipped to fly on short sightseeing jaunts or hunting trips? It had no battery or radio. In addition, I had to carry extra cans of fuel and a fuel pump in my back seat in order to travel the distance.

My incentive was a new assignment at Tanana Alaska Native Service Hospital. This promotion transfer came after completing my two-year term at the Anchorage hospital. It also followed soul-searching and possibility-seeking by Ruby and myself. The Mission Covenant group and a Baptist group presented the need for a medical missionary at Nome, Alaska. Since mission work was our original goal for my medical work, these challenges attracted us, yet there were also possibilities within the other Alaskan Public Health hospitals. After much consideration, I realized that because of the nature of my work, I would be a "missionary doctor," regardless of the agency. Therefore, I turned in my requests to Public Health. First choice: Tanana, sole doctor and administrator; second choice: Dillingham, west in Bristol Bay above the Alaska Peninsula, two or three physicians; third choice: Bethel, also west, but along the Kuskokwim River, four physicians.

Now the wait was over and Tanana was mine—if I could get there. I'd carefully studied the aeronautical charts and plotted my course. I didn't file an official flight plan since Tanana hospital knew I was coming, and I'd left a map marking out my intended route with Ruby and Paul Carlson.

In the process of moving to Tanana, I was transfering the J-3. Ruby and the children would arrive later on a commercial flight.

Moving to Tanana was quite a process all right. We'd bought $1,000 worth of staple goods such as flour, sugar, coffee, shortening, and laundry detergent. We had to mark, address, and haul all this to the railroad station, where it would be transported to Nenana. From there, it would travel by sternwheeler barge down the muddy Yukon River to Tanana, where our boxes along with many others would be dropped onto the shore for us to locate and claim. I was just beginning to understand the significance of this intervillage river highway that carried life to the villages that clung to the its banks.

I thought most of the process-problems were over as I flew along, easily finding my checkpoints, beginning with the Susitna River below me and the railroad securely to my right. Soon Talkeetna slipped beneath me. Next came Curry. The railroad cut through some mountains about 4,500 feet tall, curving around small blue mountain lakes cradled in the deep green valleys. When I came out on the other side of the mountain into a flat valley, I saw billowing white clouds. I was a neophyte pilot, but I knew better than to mess with a thunderstorm. I would need a Plan B.

The question was, what is Plan B? I pulled out my map and considered going around the thunderstorm, but Summit with Windy Pass was the only pass to the north. I didn't want to backtrack. I looked around me. With a floatplane, Alaska's lakes provided unlimited landing opportunities. There waiting for me was the answer: a 3,000 foot lake.

I quickly dropped down and, with a swoosh of sparkling spray, landed. Jumping out and into the water with my hipboots—(constant attire for a float plane-pilot)—I towed the plane over the marshy grass and near to an incoming stream with a sandy beach. Pulling out my fishing rod, I cast my shiny artifical lure into the area where the icy clear water melted into the dark lake.

On my second cast, my rod suddenly jerked and the fight was on. After several minutes of playing with the fish, bringing it in, letting the rod spin out, and then bringing it in again, I pulled in what appeared to be a large rainbow trout. I measured it past my knee—about 22 inches—larger than any rainbow I'd ever seen. I cast again and again. Nearly every other cast brought in a trout 20 to 24 inches long. I'd fished around Anchorage but never encountered success like this. This was paradise! Unfortunately, I had no means to preserve my catch, and I knew I wouldn't be going anywhere soon, so I released all but one fish.

Toward the north, in my air pathway, I could still see the magnificent thunderstorm, with clouds shoving against one another until they pushed higher and higher in the sky. Around the dark edges of this energy pile, lightening flashed, warning me not to enter the canyon.

I'd learned from earlier trips, such as the moose hunt, to take along emergency gear. I dug around in the plane until I found a lightweight skillet. Being a Good Boy scout, I always carried matches, and soon a merry fire crackled on the sandy shore in the early evening summer light. I thought "fish" would be a logical menu choice, and sure enough, it was large enough that I didn't have to worry about an appetizer or dessert. I had remembered to add "tent" to my emergency gear list, and after pushing several rocks out of the way, pounded down the stakes. Before settling in for an overnight campout, I disposed of my fish bones—away from my campsite. If a bear needed an appetizer or dessert, I didn't want to be on its menu.

Before heading into the confines of my tent, I sat beside my flickering fire, taking in the remote beauty of the evening shadows reflecting on the lake framed by tall spruce trees. I felt content. My stomach was full, I had a fish tale, my floatplane gently rocked nearby, and here I was in this awesome land that exceeded my dreams. Times like this reminded me to stop and thank the Creator for his magnificent handiwork. It also made me forget the winter when the sun lurked below the horizon and every living thing crouched together against the cold.

Fortunately, my campout was interrupted only by brief rain squalls and wind batting at my tent—not a bear. By morning, the storm had dissipated and I returned to Plan A, following the railway over Cantwell to the purple mountainsides of Mt. McKinley Park, above Healy and Ferry. There I let go of my railroad security blanket and launched off into the wilderness, taking a compass heading straight for Tanana.

In March, I'd visited Tanana to check out the 35-bed hospital and the village. Dr. Hamill took me around the attractive medical facilities, which included a white with red trim, two-story, coal-burning hospital, adjacent nurses quarters, and two new two-bedroom duplexes. The river, a mile across with an island in the middle, was an easy stone's throw from the duplexes.

Over the course of my two-week stay, we toured the village and met some of the people. The main street, "Front" street, originated about seven miles west of the village at a cliff overlooking the winter-aged ice on the river. From there it traveled upriver and down a hill into the green-roofed, clean-white housing where the CAA employees lived near the airstrip, and toward the medical complex. The airstrip extended behind both the CAA area and the hospital.

The road, more like a wide bike path, served only the antiquated red ambulance, several CAA vehicles, and the Distant Early Warning (DEW) station trucks. We planned to say goodbye to our faithful Chevy, since most people walked the short distance to wherever they needed to go.

Next came the old-fashioned, sagging white frame two-room schoolhouse. Anna Bortel, an enthusiastic single schoolteacher bubbled over with questions when she heard our family was moving to Tanana. The schoolteachers, CAA personnel, DEW employees, some of the hospital staff, and missionaries were the primary non-native people in the village. Near the school outhouses, "Back" street appeared with one- and two-room cabins standing behind the buildings, which seemed to be tossed out along Front Street. The sled dog's houses, next to many of these cabins, served more as look-out stations for the dogs, who seemed to prefer standing on top of these houses and howling in unison or harmony.

Front Street moved past the school and before a large two-story house owned by a white man who had married an Indian woman, then up to the general store where sporadically flown-in fruits and vegetables were anemic in color and exorbitant in price. The road dipped slightly and ran past the dark evergreen Episcopal Church. The Arctic Missions house-chapel followed next. I met the congenial missionaries, Roy and Marge Gronning, a study in contrasts since he was over six feet tall, and she not even five feet. Near this point, Back Street disappeared into narrow dogsled trails among clumps of willows.

Undaunted by the thawing and freezing of the Alaskan springtime, the main road continued for nearly eight more miles, past enormous gravel pits, a cemetery with occasional crosses poking through the snow near the old Episcopal Church site, and then up into the hills to the DEW station, or "White Alice" as the villagers called it. The purpose of this DEW station, and the more than 50 other manned stations that extended north of the United States and Canada, was to throw up an invisible electronic barrier across the polar skies and the roof of the North American continent.

This modern defense system made me think of the changes this many-named locality had known in its history since the 1800s. In 1899, Captain Charles Steward Farnsworth brought his wife and young son here to "Fort Gibbon," where he found a fort composed mostly of tents, incomplete barracks, and lean-tos. I couldn't believe anyone could spend an arctic winter in those conditions. Farnsworth rented a one-room log shack with a leaky sod roof. This inadequate barrack became the center of social activities for the enlisted men and upriver natives, who would crowd into the room to eat dessert and listen to Helen Farnsworth play piano while her black cook sang.

Until 1925, this outpost, along with four others in Alaska, maintained law and order during the gold rush. Prior to this time, traders and natives knew the location by the name of *Nuklukoyet* or, "place where the two rivers meet." In 1869, the Alaska Commercial Company absorbed the Pioneer Company's trading post there and called the village Tanana Station. I'd heard that at one time 3,000 people lived at this location; now the village had a count of around 110.

I liked what I saw in this village, which blended non-native and Indian cultures, and I felt confident that living here would satisfy me and cure my "Alaskan Fever."

I'd flown with another bush pilot on my first trip to Tanana. Now I was off on my own. Before I had left Anchorage, CAA weather briefing advised me of forest fires, started by lightning during the extremely dry season. I expected to see billowing black smoke or yellow-orange flashes of fire. I saw neither, but I smelled the smoke. Even though I knew of the forest fires, my immediate reaction to the acrid odor was fear—fear of fire in the plane. Startled, I looked around and then focused on the strange haze before me.

The haze was not just a cloudy weather condition—it was actually smoke from the forest fires. Although it was about 10:00 A.M., the sky wrapped me in an eerie gray-brown veil. At first, the sun appeared haloed in a brown shiny ring, but then as if controlled by a dimmer switch, the sun gradually faded from sight. If it weren't for the sensation of dry heat, the smoke could have been mistaken for damp fog. Forward visibility deteriorated rapidly from five miles to two miles. I turned my neck downward where visibility remained the same.

Landmark checkpoints disappeared as the rivers and lakes below me all looked alike, with the low spruce-covered hills rolling and repeating themselves beneath me. I wanted to trust my compass heading, but something seemed wrong. Later I learned that this area was noted for severe magnetic variations. The smoke crowded around me until I had only one-

Assignment: Tanana 55

mile forward visibility. An hour passed. Somewhere I'd missed my main checkpoint, the Kantishna River. Where was I?

Added to this dilemma, my gas tank showed empty. The gas tank could be refilled from the cockpit inserting a rubber hose into the five-gallon gas cans in my baggage compartment and pumping out the gas into the nose tank with my wobble pump. This procedure required some tricky maneuvering within the cockpit.

With that accomplished, I needed to find Plan C for getting on course and to Tanana. At this point, Plan C was Common Sense, not Compass. I chose the first small stream and followed it downstream. Eventually all running water in this area would wind up in the Tanana River. Even in all this smoke, the Tanana River could not be missed, since it was over 600 miles long and averaged 200 to 400 feet wide, with many side channels and sloughs. Since it was the Yukon's largest tributary, it would surely lead me to my destination.

In any case, I now felt as though I was finally getting somewhere, despite my confusion. After awhile, a large river came into view and as I followed it for several miles, I was able to identify Manley Hot Springs. Apparently, I'd followed the Zitziana River to the Tanana River. I straightened my tired neck, looked ahead, and easily found my way along the wide, winding river. Once again, I could check off the landmarks.

About an hour past Manley Hot Springs, I crossed off my last checkpoint, the confluence of the Tanana and Yukon rivers. Right on target and three miles past this point, I spotted Tanana, a beautiful sight for smoke-filled eyes.

After circling the village and checking out the river along the shore in front of the hospital, I splashed down on the legendary Yukon River. Several of the hospital personnel ran out to meet me as I taxied against the current up to shore.

It felt good to be here and I looked forward to starting my official duties. Nevertheless, I was glad that it was Saturday night. I could use a day of rest before getting into the swing of things.

8
A strange village welcome
July 1957

Sickness seemed out of place as summer saturated the air and permeated every corner of the Tanana hospital. Right at this moment, there were no surgeries, emergencies, or babies born, so I felt relaxed as I leisurely walked through the vacant waiting room onto the hospital's front porch. Hanging pots of red and white petunias flounced in the gentle breeze and created a friendly greeting to any prospective patients.

Across the dusty road, where several children stirred up the powdery surface with their bicycles, our garden flourished on the riverbank, surrounded by a hedge of pink, yellow, and lavender sweet peas. The Natives shook their heads at Ruby's attempt to grow tomatoes, but encouraged her with the cabbages, peas, and carrots.

A strange village welcome

Behind this plot, the swift, muddy Yukon hurried down toward the sea, while a "kicker" boat fought the current and buzzed up the river. This sound mixed with the persistent and repetitive whine of a chain saw. Already, this felt like home. My family had adjusted to village life, and I felt comfortable with the hospital routine.

I hadn't always felt this way. I remembered my strange village welcome last July, when I was abruptly brought into the swing of things.

"Doctor! Doctor!" The cacaphony of words and door-pounding had finally turned into intelligible sounds. I had rolled over in bed and looked at the clock: 5:00 A.M. This was Sunday and my first morning in Tanana.

"What do they want?" I asked myself, climbing out of bed. And who were "they"? I was alone without my family for this first week, and the silent duplex did not yield any answers to my questions. When my curiosity overcame my apprehension, I warily tiptoed to the back door.

"This is the doctor. What do you want?" I asked through the door, trying to sound calm.

"Simon killed John," a voice stood out amidst the clamor.

And that was my welcome to Tanana. At that moment, I felt awkward and unprepared to work with these villagers. Now, nearly a year later, I was accustomed to village life and knew what to anticipate. For instance, I suspected it was unsafe to walk on Back Street on Saturday nights because of the drinking and resulting fights. This was also the case, after potlaches, or the Spring Carnival, or the Fourth of July celebration.

I thought about these unique celebrations, which we so much enjoyed, and how we were the first doctor's family to participate in the potlaches held at the community hall. We hadn't been sure what to expect our first time. Benches lined the perimeter of the community hall and two barrel stoves squatted on the recently scrubbed splintery board floor. The villagers, who arrived at 6:00 P.M., seated themselves on the benches. Five-foot- wide oil-cloth runners were spread before these benches and the latecomers then sat on the opposite edges facing the benches. We brought our own bowls and spoons for the greasy soup, which was ladled from a sawed-in-half gas barrel and served by men walking down the center of our oilcloth "table." This "serving bowl" reminded me of our livestock watering barrels back on the farm. The soup's content varied depending on the donated meat and other items. Often we could expect a mix of canned vegetables and macaroni—and only a little salt.

After the soup, we were served meat—usually moose and sometimes caribou. The servers cut off custom-size chunks, depending on the size and age of the individual. In most cases, the fist-size serving was eaten with fingers and a knife. Very carefully, the meat was bitten with the teeth and then the knife was used to cut it off dangerously near one's lips. Amazingly, I never had to suture any faces as a result of this procedure.

Our meal progressed on to pilot bread, a thick, four-inch round, saltless cracker; butter; strong, hot tea; canned peaches or fruit cocktail; gum from the general store; and cigarettes.

We didn't want to set ourselves apart from the Natives, and these were good times for us to mingle. On several occasions, I took the chief hunting with my plane for potlach meat.

The Spring Carnival in April provided another opportunity for our family to learn about village customs. School was dismissed and Natives from surrounding villages joined in the celebration. The frozen river furnished a slushy arena for the dogsled and snowshoe races. Men, women, and children had their own categories, with women often doing better than the men since they didn't drink.

The riverbank hot dog stand seemed out of place and more appropriate for a baseball game, but the Native man managing it did a thriving business. Ruby, the schoolteachers, and the missionaries took turns volunteering to sell refreshments at this main attraction.

Ruby and I also participated in the Fourth of July, races which included activities such as sack races, bike races, egg-carrying races, and field events. Ruby, running with an egg on a spoon from the general store to the parish hall, came in second and won $3.00. I surprised the villagers by placing first in the broad jump, winning $5.00.

All this familiarity, however, was unknown to me on that first day in Tanana when I heard the men knocking and the voice telling me that Simon had killed John.

"Now John's friends want to shoot Simon," another man's voice added to the previous headliner.

Finally, I realized that my life was not in danger, so I opened the door and found three Indian men crowded on my back porch steps. Their brown eyes were wide with alarm, and they pressed me for a plan to prevent the lynching.

"Let me get dressed," I said, stalling for time. "Then take me to your chief."

I'd looked forward to coming to this village, and I'd expected to juggle the many hats of medical administrator, field physician, and public relations officer. I hadn't bargained for this last responsibility: justice of the peace.

After only a few moments, the Natives impatiently knocked on the door and urged me to hurry. We walked a short distance along Back Street. This was not exactly how I imagined meeting the chief. When we arrived at his cabin, the young chief, Alfred Grant, introduced himself. We put aside social chit-chat and got right to the point. Together we decided that the only way to prevent further violence was to hold the murderer in a cabin guarded by four men.

The chief and the men who had escorted me, left the cabin to implement the plan. I returned to the hospital and with the two-way radio summoned the Fairbanks U.S. troopers for assistance.

Now standing on the hospital porch on this beautiful summer day, I remembered my apprehension about telling Ruby about my village initiation. How would this affect her first impressions of life in Tanana? As it turned out, Ruby took it in stride and plunged into adapting to village life. I was proud of her hardiness, management skills, and capabilities as she mastered the tasks of daily living in the village.

For instance, in Tanana, food provisions were more limited than in Anchorage, and Ruby constantly had to plan ahead. Our enormous final grocery shopping trip in Anchorage helped us make it through the first winter, but in early spring we had to place another order, which would also be brought in by barge. It was not an easy chore to figure out how many canned fruits and vegetables, boxes of cereal, jello, cake mixes, instant potatoes, and powdered milk, the family would consume over the course of the year.

Sternwheeler barges delivered all this grocery shopping to the river shore, where the boxes were dumped on the sand and left for villagers to identify by family name. The village shook as the barges approached from upriver.

Food preparation was complicated by the lack of fresh fruits, vegetables, dairy products, and baked goods. Consequently,

Ruby baked nearly every day and became quite proficient at shaping hot dog and hamburger buns for summer picnics. With culinary ingenuity, she took powdered items and wild meat and presented us with bon appétit delights. I supplemented her limited resources by infrequent medical trips to Fairbanks. Each time I left, the family eagerly scribbled out a grocery list. Ruby craved fried potatoes, so I brought her potatoes and cottage cheese. Ruth begged for bananas, and Naomi devoured the store-bought white bread. Mark had no preferences, and I bought myself bologna.

Clothes posed another challenge. We ordered them by mail from Sears, which took several weeks for a package to arrive. We were never sure what we would get. Sometimes items would be substituted or the clothes represented in the pictures didn't always look the same in real life. The girls seemed fascinated by the procedure for shoe purchases, which consisted of choosing a shoe style from the catalog, tracing around each foot, and mailing this information into Sears.

On several occasions during the year, Ruby and the children did fly to Anchorage via Fairbanks, and what a shopping spree they had. Not only did they purchase fresh fruits and vegetables, and clothes, but all the odds and ends not available in the general store or even catalog, such as sewing machine needles, clothes patterns, glue, gift wrap, and birthday cards.

Ruby's social life helped her make it through the long, dark winter. She had regular game nights at our house with the nurses and a sewing group, which included CAA and White Alice women. Our house became a revolving door for missionaries isolated along the river and for the single schoolteachers, who for a while even lived with us.

Yes, Ruby had done well with this village life, and so had the children. Naomi's closest friend was an Indian girl, Sally Wood. Although some of the Native girls would tell Sally, "Don't play with her; she's not one of us," Sally remained a loyal friend. The girls would bake cookies, play with dolls at our house, or go over to Sally's house in the summer.

Naomi watched as Sally's mother adeptly sliced fish, leaving them to hang unprotected from the rain, ravens, and flies from drying racks made of thick spruce poles. The recently caught fish shone a bright oily red, while the older fish were dark with slightly curled edges. Naomi was intrigued by Sally's "earrings" of tiny dried spruce needles, and although she didn't ask for earrings herself, she did let her hair grow into similar long braids.

Naomi and Ruth joined the 51 students in the two-room dilapidated Tanana Day School, which was later condemned in spring due to the numerous earthquakes. To keep warm they dressed like the Natives and wore red fox ruffed parkas and soft moose-skin mukluks and mittens. The mittens were attached to a braided yarn harness, which they wore over their shoulders. This device prevented the exasperation of constantly misplaced children's mittens.

I hoped my children would benefit in years to come from their experiences with Alaskan village life. As for my village experiences, I was relieved when my first unofficial day at work came to an end and the U.S. trooper showed up.

In a strange parade, Chief Alfred Grant, the murderer, and many of the Natives proceeded to the airstrip with the dead man. As the plane took off and headed back to Fairbanks, the murderer found himself with an odd seating companion: his victim.

That had been a strange day for me as well, and I was glad my welcome and initiation were over. It was, nevertheless, a clue as to what life as a village doctor would be like.

9
House calls Alaskan style
February 1958

The winter of 1958 would not release its hold on us, and for weeks the arctic temperatures hovered between 40 and 50 degrees below zero. The cold crept under window sills and around door jams, following and finding every living thing. On rare, clear days, the darkness would lift for several hours, allowing us freedom from our winter box. Not many ventured outside, and the silence accompanying the dark cold was broken only by sled dogs howling in chorus atop their houses or by the whine of a chain saw finding fuel to fight off the cold.

On this particular day, I maintained my normal routine, and by noon I'd examined a woman with tuberculosis, children with draining ears, and a large number of people with respiratory infections. Taking a break from face-to-face patient contact, I made my daily radio contact with the villages both up and down the Yukon River. Missionaries and schoolteachers usually could handle the typical medical needs, but I soon realized that this was not to be a usual day.

"Doc, Charlie's awfully sick." The Manley Hot Springs' innkeeper's voice crackled on the other end of the two-way. "He didn't show up for several days, so we checked up on him. Seems he's had stomach problems in the past, and it must be acting up 'cause there's blood everywhere. I mean, Doc, it's on his clothes, his bed, the floor . . . Doc?"

"Sounds like a bleeding stomach ulcer." I tried to calm him as I considered possible medical treatment.

"I'm afraid we're going to lose him." The innkeeper provided more details.

"Try to give him some broth, tea, jello, or powdered milk." I felt helpless at this distance and was stalling, trying to think of ways to treat Charlie.

"Doc, I wish *you* could come." The innkeeper started to plead, but then added more dismal information. "The weather's bad and nothing's flying."

Here, the ice fog had dissipated and in its place, the warmer temperatures of -10 F brought snow squalls.

"Why don't you contact Fairbanks to get a plane to come in for medical evacuation," I advised. Uncertain of that possibility and sensing the urgency of the situation, I added, "Meanwhile, I'll try to scoot under these squalls and get in."

I felt caught between the need to attend this seriously ill man and to stay at the Tanana hospital, where I expected a young woman to go into labor at any time. I talked over the situation with the nurses, and they assured me that they could take care of the delivery if necessary.

I knew these bush nurses could handle nearly any situation, but still I felt apprehensive as I headed over to check my plane.

I tried to keep my plane prepared for these kinds of emergencies. A 150-foot extension cord trailed from the house, across the road, and down the 12-foot bank to the J-3 on skis. This umbilical cord supported a 200-watt bulb tucked into the plane engine, which in turn was wrapped in blankets and canvas: at these immobilizing temperatures, my plane was ready to go.

It was already after 12:30 P.M. and I only had two more hours of daylight. I needed 45 minutes of flying time, yet I moved quickly. My emergency medical supplies were in readiness for these kinds of mercy flights, and sleeping bag, axe, gun, engine cover, one-burner Coleman stove with four-inch stove pipe to funnel heat under the cowling, and food were on the plane. The CAA weather report indicated marginal flying conditions, and I realized that setting down en route was a probability.

After a routine preflight check, I took off on the rough river ice. Once I'd climbed to 500 feet, I followed the Yukon for a mile and then continued up the Tanana River. There was a moderate chop over Squaw Crossing as the wind funneled through a saddle in the hills to the north. Visibility was poor but adequate as I clung to the north bank of the river.

The tension in my neck eased as landmarks indicated that I was only fifteen minutes out of Manley. Then, without warning, oil splattered up over my windshield! I glanced down at the oil pressure and engine temperature. Normal. What was wrong? Oil continued to ooze out of the right cowling and within minutes my forward visibility was zero.

Out my side windows, I searched for an emergency landing spot on the river. Soft new snow deceptively smoothed over the treacherous pressure heaves formed by the tug-of-war between churning water and restricting ice. When the water would win, huge sheets of ice would break and push diagonally above the other river ice. Only an occasional jagged edge, however, poked through the snow, revealing the danger.

Aware of the odds, I selected a reasonably smooth area, reduced the power, and settled in for the softest approach I could make. In protest to this landing, the plane bounced against the chunks of ice and finally jolted to a stop.

Cautiously, I crawled out of the plane. The skis were still firmly attached to the aircraft—a positive sign. Trying to avoid the messy oil, I loosened the cowling. What a dirty sight. But more good news: three quarts of oil remained—enough to make it to my destination. And then I found the culprit, a dislodged oil cap. I screwed it on easily.

Cleaning the windshield was not so simple. I scraped the now snow-glazed molasses-like oil from the windshield and then used snow to finish the cleaning process. Visibility was down to a mile now and I needed to get back into the air. Scouting ahead on the river, I checked over my best takeoff path, then resumed flight to Manley.

The rest of the flight was uneventful, and my thoughts

turned to the history of Manley Hot Springs. Manley had a flow of hot water comparable to Chena Hot Springs and sat beside the Tanana River, about 90 miles west of Fairbanks. The location was easily accessible by water, and a trading post was established there in 1881. In 1901, a prospector, J.F. Karshner, homesteaded the spring site. Thousands of hopeful miners flooded the area when other prospectors struck gold in the nearby Eureka and Tofty areas.

One of these men, Frank Manley, differed from the empty-pocketed others: already he had several hundred thousand dollars. Consequently, Manley's money and Karshner's hot springs soon joined hands to start Alaska's first substantial geothermal resource project. This fortuitous relationship encountered one snag when word got out that Manley's real name was William Beaumont. Accused of horse thievery, he'd left Texas and assumed an alias. Sent back to his homeland, he was acquitted and returned to Manley.

Beaumont, alias Manley, and Karshner cleared land for farming and built a sixty-room hotel, along with other buildings for raising poultry, hogs, and dairy cattle. In 1910, the future held promise and Manley had a booming population of 101 people. Mining, however, declined, and then in 1913, the hotel burned down, ending this glorious era of Manley Hot Springs' history. By 1930, only 45 residents remained. Now, in 1958, the village of half Natives and half white, vacillated between 20 and 30 people, depending on the hunting and fishing seasons.

"Doc, so glad you make it!" the innkeeper greeted me after my plane engine shuttered into silence. "Ol' Charlie isn't doing well at all. He can't eat, can't get out of bed . . . boy, am I glad to see you."

The innkeeper tied the plane down as I drained the remaining oil into a two-gallon can. Snowflakes clumped together and began to blanket the plane. There was no cord here to sustain life while the plane waited for my return. Carrying the oil with me, I tried to find out more about Charlie from the innkeeper.

"Well, Doc, he's one of the ol' timers. Been in Alaska since somewhere about 1880—you know, when all the others came up to the Last Frontier with gold fever. He's an independent and tough old codger—a survivor. Worked on the road from Fairbanks to Rampart, mined gold around the Eureka area, and of course homesteaded, too.

We reached the innkeeper's two-story roadhouse, which provided eating facilities, a lounge, general store, and upstairs sleeping accommodations. A shed housing the generator joined the several houses clustering around the roadhouse. Several hundred yards farther I could see the steam rising from the hot springs, with the schoolhouse, teacher's quarters, and a small bath house nestled near the warmth.

I tried to keep pace with the innkeeper, my slick-bottomed "bunny boots" slipped on the hard-packed snow as I followed him off the main trail towards one of the houses adjacent the roadhouse.

"Yep, that ol' fellow's at least 85 years old. Been here in Manley Hot Springs for about fifteen or so years—everyone likes him . . . Poor guy, doesn't seem to have any family, though." The innkeeper seemed to know a lot about Charlie, probably a lot about everyone in Manley Hot Springs.

"That's Charlie's place. You should see his garden in the summer. Big ol' cabbages, plenty of carrots, and piles of potatoes . . ."

It appeared that Charlie was upholding the Manley Hot Springs' legend, beginning in 1910 when 150 tons of potatoes were shipped downriver to the Iditerod mining district.

" . . . things wouldn't be the same without Charlie around."

Yes, Charlie sounded like a lively character, although right now there didn't seem to be much life in the cabin in front of us. The windows stared back at us blankly, and only a thin thread of smoke coming from a crooked stovepipe blended into the early afternoon dusky sky. At 2:00 P.M. the sun was going down.

Climbing up the several steps to his porch, we stomped the snow off our boots—a kind of notice that we had arrived.

Tugging open the door, we walked into a dark cold room. The paling outdoor light did not penetrate the room and only a dim kerosene lamp flickered on the faded oilcloth-covered table. Three heavy wooden chairs grouped around this small, sturdy table, and wooden shelves nearby displayed a meager assortment of canned goods, pancake mix, a round box of oatmeal, and half-empty bottle of syrup. Slowly my eyes adjusted to the darkness and I set the two-gallon can of plane oil on the flat top of the barrel stove.

As I approached a low metal army bunkbed against one wall,

the putrid smell of vomit confronted me. There was Charlie. Our eyes met in the darkness.

"Charlie, I'm Doctor Gaede from Tanana. I came to help you."

Charlie, weak but conscious, nodded.

The innkeeper pumped up the kerosene lamp, which brightened the room. I could see dried vomit on Charlie's flannel shirt, army blanket, and the floor around his bed.

"Charlie, you're looking pretty rough. Tell me what happened."

"Well, Doc," he began feebly, "I've had stomach trouble before and had some bleeding a couple years ago . . ." He rested a moment before continuing." I saw a doc in Fairbanks and he gave me some medicine, which cleared it up. Now lately I've had stomach pains again and not much appetite . . . The past couple days I've been throwing up everything I eat."

Gently pushing his blankets to one side, I began my examination. The shriveled skin of his large-boned arm folded into the blood pressure cuff. His blood pressure was down to 80/40 with a faint rapid pulse of 120. Carefully, I rearranged his flannel shirt, exposing skin drawn tightly over prominent ribs and a slightly bloated stomach. Yes, his stomach was tender . . . liver barely perceptible . . . heart and lungs o.k. He was larger than I first thought, probably six feet, but only about 150 pounds.

My eyes had adjusted to the dim room, and focusing back on his face, I saw stubs of teeth, coated with dark, dried blood, contrasting with ghost-white skin. The diagnosis was obvious: hemorrhaging gastric ulcer.

"All right, Charlie, let's see what we can do to make you more comfortable." Our work was cut out for us.

While I had been examining Charlie, the innkeeper had stoked up the fire in the barrel stove and started heating water. Now he began cleaning up the cabin, locating clean bedding, clothes, and towels. In the process, he found some canned soup and warmed that on the stove, also.

Meanwhile, I tended to Charlie, starting an IV and giving him the requested "pain shot."

The innkeeper returned to his inn, and I fed Charlie spoonfuls of soup broth. In a short while, the innkeeper came back, announcing, "I got through to Fairbanks on the radio, but they're socked in and planes aren't moving. You won't get any help from there tonight, or until the ice fog lifts."

"It's o.k. Doc, I've lived a full life—I'm ready to meet my Maker." Sensing my concern, Charlie tried to reassure me. IF we could just pull Charlie through tonight, we'd be o.k. but, it could be a long night.

After giving Charlie two bottles of IV, he became more comfortable and his vital signs stabilized. The three of us began exchanging Alaskan stories of our experiences, eventually all falling to sleep, the Innkeeper and me in makeshift beds.

Suddenly, I was awake. Something *was* wrong. Like a mother sensing trouble with a child, I got up to check on Charlie. The flickering kerosene lamp cast gentle shadows on his peaceful face. I checked his blood pressure and pulse. Something was wrong: Charlie was going into shock.

I'd used up my two bottles of IV solution. Now I'd have to improvise. The water in the bucket on the stove was still warm, and at one time had been to a boil. Hurriedly I filled an empty IV bottle with the water, added one teaspoon of salt from the lone salt shaker on the table, and dashed out the door to cool the saline solution in the below zero snow. Moments later, both my wool-socked feet and the homemade solution were lukewarm, and I returned to my patient, quickly finding the vein and beginning the IV.

I waited. Slowly the bottle emptied and I prepared a second in similar fashion as the first. Finally, the blood pressure was perceivable, and I slowed down the IV drip. Minutes stretched into hours as I kept the night watch while the innkeeper snored unperturbed.

About 10:00 A.M., dawn pushed its way through the frigid darkness and into the cabin. Returning from a second call to Fairbanks, the innkeeper's grin gave away the good news.

"The weather's breaking! Chances are we'll have a plane by noon!"

Charlie tenaciously clung to life as he waited for the rescue plane and then endured the 40-minute flight to Fairbanks. Later I learned that once he arrived at the hospital, he received a whalloping eight units in blood tranfusions.

As Charlie's plane took off, I put my arm around the innkeeper. "Thanks for standing by me."

"Yeh, Doc," he answered gruffly. "Up here we have to stick together and make do with what we have."

Thanks to the heated engine oil I'd kept on the stove, the plane seemed eager to return home, putting on its best behavior. There were no unexpected surprises such as that earlier oil leak. Fresh snow covered the river, which yielded no trace of the previous emergency landing. In contrast, I knew that the crisis with Charlie would leave its mark on me. I thanked God for the opportunities and abilities He had blessed me with—and flew back to check on the pregnant woman.

You see, this was no ordinary pregnant woman. This was an Eskimo woman offering her child for adoption—and we were to be the parents of the gift. I was both disappointed and elated to discover that in my absence, our Mishal had entered the world and our lives.

And Charlie? Even though he may have figured his full life was complete, his body fought back anyway, granting him several more years at Manley Hot Springs.

In 1915, geologist G.A. Waring visited Manley Hot Springs and noted two main springs: one with a temperature of 52° C (125° F) and a flow of 110 gallons per minute, the other with a temperature of 58 degrees C (136° F) and a flow of 35 gallons per minute. In 1981, geophysical surveys measured the flow from the main group of springs as 374 gallons per minute. Manley Hot Springs from Energy Alaska *by Neil Davis, 1984*

Today, Manley Hot Springs continues to greet people with the same hospitality that the Innkeeper showed Dr. Gaede in 1958. Located on mile 157, the end of the Elliott Highway, west of Fairbanks, the Manley Roadhouse offers old-fashioned warmth with family-style meals, a trading post, cabins, store, gas and a small museum. There is a public campground near the bridge in town, and daily air service to and from Fairbanks.

10
King of the Arctic
March 1958

In a matter of seconds, the J-3 rapidly lost 1000 feet of altitude as a down draft-sucked it toward the coastline along the upper edge of Alaska. White-capped waves lashed out at our landmark shoreline that met the low 500- to 800-foot hills from where the tremendous unstable wind emanated. The tiny J-3 was no match for the severe winds and in spite of full throttle, I could not hold the plane on course.

"We've got to get out of here!" I yelled to Leonard Lane, a large Eskimo, who was folded into my small back-seat. We had just left Point Hope, which was home to Leonard, even though he worked at the Tanana hospital. I turned the plane with the wind and let it drift away from the hills and toward the rough open water, where in contrast the air remained stable. The plane temporarily leveled off, but the next twenty minutes were a nightmare.

The howling wind increased in velocity and hurled gusts of snow down the barren hillsides and up into the air. At the same time, ice fog from the open ocean water gathered in patches around us. Wind whistled through the cracks in the plane's door and sent shivers down our backs as the temperature dropped from 20° F to 0° F. After 15 minutes of this buffeting we were down to 200 feet, searching for a point of reference and finding only sparse tufts of brown shoreline grass. New snow fell rapidly. The grass vanished. White out.

Panic grabbed me. I figured we'd bury ourselves in a plane coffin. But before giving up the fight, I said a fast prayer and decided to backtrack to where I'd last seen the grass markers. I sharply banked the plane, all the time hoping that I wouldn't become disoriented and fly the plane into the ground. As if a hand briefly lifted the white curtain, I could distinguish dark spots.

"See the grass, Doc!" shouted Leonard. "Level us out!"

We discovered ourselves over a lake crowded next to the shoreline hills. The raging blizzard allowed us no time to circle the "landing strip" or do a touch-and-go to test the landing conditions. I couldn't waste any time. I lowered the plane into the white blowing expanse, uncertain of the altitude and having little depth perception. The 40 mph crosswinds threw the plane off balance, and it hit hard on one ski, then skidded into and bounced off the hidden drifts near the lake's edge. Even though we were down, adrenaline coursed through my body in readiness to continue the fight against nature.

We were still not secure. The wind shoved the plane around, as we dug around in the two-foot snow for tie-downs. Without losing sight of the plane, Leonard struggled toward the barren lake edge to explore the possibilities, then improvised an anchor by packing a bundle of twigs deep into the snow.

At 2:30 P.M., somewhere north of Kivalina, we squeezed back into the plane to wait out the storm. Before long, the claustrophobic white faded into darkness and we packed our sleeping bags around us. All night the 60 mph winds hurled around us, and the plane trembled like a leaf.

Sleep eluded us as we shifted our positions, trying to stretch our confined bodies. There was plenty of time to think—and even to talk, if we raised our voices.

"Hey, Doc. Looks as if your dream turned into a nightmare!" said Leonard.

"We've sure had our troubles," I replied.

For the past three years I'd dreamed of an encounter with the king of the Arctic: a polar bear. Leonard, had volunteered to guide me on this expedition. For three weeks prior to the actual trip, we'd checked our aviation charts and flight gear, experimented with engine heating equipment, and discussed how to spot a polar bear.

"I know it sounds impossible to find a white bear on white ice," Leonard had said in one of his informal teaching sessions. "But they are usually spotted by their shadow and their yellow color."

Much to the delight of my children, we practiced arctic survival and built an "igloo" out of the crusty snow along the riverbank. Leonard showed me how to cut the large snow blocks and balance them inward and upward in a dome. Unlike the myth that Eskimos lived in these snow houses, the igloos were used for temporary outdoor survival, much like a tent.

"Doc, we've done all we can," said Leonard one evening. "Now it's time for the real thing."

On March 8, we soared off into the crystal clear dawn. A 20 to 30 mph tail wind gaily pushed us down the well-marked course of the Yukon to our first stop, Galena. So far, so good. We refueled, then set our course over unfamiliar country of rolling hills.

Finding our next checkpoint, Selawik, was like playing hide-and-go-seek among the flat look-alike lakes in the vast whiteness. Even the Selawik River hid from us. After sometime, and dropping to a lower altitude, we picked out the village and landed on the river in front of the village. As in all the villages, a plane's arrival was a highlight, and villagers greeted us, plying us with questions about the Who, What, Wheres of ourselves.

After stretching our legs, we compacted ourselves back into the plane and flew a short distance to Noorvik. Once again we landed, this time on the Kobuk River in front of the village. About 50 curious rosy-cheeked Eskimo children surrounded us with their smiles and shy laughter. We stayed an hour, drinking thick, hot coffee and visiting with some of Leonard's relatives.

Another skip and a jump and we were at Kotzebue. I remembered my first experiences there with the tundra taxi. I thought of baby Andrew and pictured him as a chubby-faced child running around his village in a fur-ruffed parka and tiny mukluks. Even though that had happened only three years ago, it seemed millenniums ago in my experience and knowledge of Alaska. We didn't take time to visit there, but quickly refueled and pressed northward along the bleak arctic coastline.

White barrenness stretched in all directions as trees shrunk out of sight to our right and massive ice packs appeared to our left. Before long, we passed over the sod houses of Kivalina. There, herds of caribou were scattered across the low hills. A myriad of frozen freshwater lakes followed the coastline, separated from the salty ocean by only several hundred yards of tundra. "What's that down there by the ice crack?" asked Leonard, nudging me on my left shoulder and pointing out the window.

With hopes high, we spiraled down, only to disturb a seal, content with sunning itself until the sound of the engine's roar sent him slipping back into the water. Polar bear didn't come quite that easily.

Six hours after we'd left Tanana, we sighted our destination: the Eskimo village of Point Hope, precariously balanced on the tip of a long spit extending into the ocean. We bumped down on the snow-drifted tundra, and soon Leonard's family and friends swarmed around us.

"Doc, this is my brother, Amos," said Leonard. "He's the best hunter in the area and can give us all the latest hunting information."

"Yes, I think you've got a good chance of getting a bear," smiled Amos. "Several bear were taken just last week."

"You can stay with us," volunteered the schoolteacher, Fred Fisher, after introducing himself and his wife.

I appreciated the welcome mat and took comfort knowing that wherever I'd go in Alaska I'd never be without food, lodging, or assistance. And then now we did need some assistance.

"Leonard, what are we going to do about plane fuel," I whispered to him as we gathered in the general store where I saw only blazo and kerosene.

"Do you think the plane could fly if we'd mix blazo in with the remaining aviation fuel?" he responded.

We didn't have any other solution, so in preparation for the next day's hunt we hauled the blazo out to the plane to refuel. I didn't like this solution, but our choices were limited. I carried some gas with me, but I hadn't anticipated this problem.

Later that evening, Don Lisbourne, president of the village, came over to the schoolhouse. "Dr. Gaede, you might be able to use the 86 octane combat gas that was left here when the army company nearby closed several years ago."

It was too late to do anything, so we waited for the morning. March 9 wakened us with a bright brisk $-8°$ F and we hurried out to drain the blazo mixture from the plane and replace it with combat gas. As we drained the tank, we found a leak in the gasoline sediment bowl. By the time this was fixed, it was already 1:00 P.M. I felt impatient to get out on the hunt, but before heading over the open water to the rough ice pack, we circled the village, testing the gas in the plane. All systems were go as the plane swallowed up the gas, running smoothly and with full power in the calm arctic air.

The hunt began. We proceeded west at about 1,000 feet along the numerous small open leads of water. Every few minutes we spotted seal, shiny dark against the white ice. They never stuck around for a close inspection, but slid into the water at the sound of the plane.

I couldn't have asked for a better guide. Leonard knew the ice and taught me about the strong old ice and thin new ice. "The old ice often appears rougher and has a gray color, but the new ice is smooth and whiter. Thin ice may appear slightly blue," he continued on with his mini-lecture. "It's often tempting to land on a large, smooth, pure white ice pad near an open lead to go after a seal or bear, but you must always remember the consequences of a plane breaking through the thin ice."

With that caution in mind, we scrutinized the area below us.

"Do you think we're near the international date line?" I asked, trying to visualize the broken map line dividing the Russian and American territories.

"I think so, Doc. Can't you see the red ice?" Leonard chuckled.

We returned to Point Hope and after refueling, played a hunch and began scouting southward near the coastline. About twelve miles west of Cape Thompson, Leonard hollered. "Doc, that's old ice ahead. We should find bear."

I let down to 500 feet as we neared the first smooth field of old ice. Suddenly, Leonard grabbed my shoulders and yelled, "There he is! Over there!"

I immediately banked the plane and took a good look. Sure enough, just ahead was a light yellow spot with a dark shadow. We made a wide circle. The bear sat back and like a dog begging for food raised his thick front feet with padded paws. Balanced in this way, his small head rotated as it followed the plane. Leonard assured me that the ice was old and could hold the plane. We landed on a flat area, downwind about a half mile from the arctic king. "Doc, these bear think nothing of swimming for hours in the frigid waters: we don't want to spook him away," Leonard informed me.

We quickly loaded our rifles and quietly crept along and over the 6- to 8-foot-high broken pressure ridges. "Which way do you think we should go, Doc?" asked Leonard in the confusing maze.

At the same instance I caught a glimpse of movement to our right. We ducked and kept under cover as we stalked our potential prize.

Unexpectedly, the bear sensed danger and began running parallel to us. He was about 300 to 400 yards away—a tough, if not impossible shot. "I'll get my sight on him," I whispered loudly to Leonard. "You yell and get his attention."

I poked my head up and I rested my 300 Magnum over an ice block, trying to get the bear in my five-power scope. Leonard also tried to focus on the bear. Then he yelled. Hesitantly, the bear stopped to look at us with his black expressionless eyes. The front half of his body was exposed past an ice block, so I squeezed off my shot.

"Good shot, Doc! You hit him," shouted Leonard as we both leaped over the pressure ridges running toward our game—all the time, Leonard attempting to focus my 8 mm camera on the bear.

The bear suddenly staggered out from behind ice blocks about 100 yards from where we had last seen him. Bright blood covered his front shoulder. Leonard stood back to photograph this arctic adventure. As I walked ahead, the white fury confronted me. Even though he was severely wounded, he defied me with open mouth and oustretched claws. I expected my next shot to end his misery, but the bullet placed in his heart area left him still fighting. After the third shot, everything became silent, except for the slow clicking of the movie camera.

The beautiful heavy silvery-white bear appeared to be about

four years old and was over eight feet from nose to tail. Long gray evening shadows crept along the pressure ridges, warning us of our limited time on the ice. Quickly we took a few more pictures then went to work. Leonard skinned while I flew the plane closer to the bear. I couldn't believe that he was nearly finished when I returned with the plane. I took out a can of gas and packed the 60- to 75-pound bear skin in the back of the plane.

The can of gas and skin were not an equal exchange. We were overloaded. We surveyed our course. Uneven ice crisscrossed by large snow drifts paralleled several two-foot-wide cracks in the ice. Climbing into the plane, we hoped for the best. I opened the throttle and the plane picked up speed. At 40 mph, we hit a snow drift that bounced us several feet into the air before we slammed back down. Immediately, we struck another large drift, which bounced us about 20 to 25 feet into the air. We still didn't have enough airspeed to remain airborne, and the plane whined in protest of the abuse.

I nearly froze at the controls when I realized we had used up most of our runway. Tall pressure ridges sprung up in front of us. Just below us, I saw three fresh ice cracks with open water. I kicked a hard right rudder before we hit the ice. The plane swung diagonally over the dangerous cracks as we bounced hard on one ski, and over to a new smooth area. I opened the plane door and looked out at the skis as I taxied a short distance. "It's a tough plane," I said to Leonard, pulling the door shut, and discovering that the door window frame had been bent.

Our second attempt at takeoff was successful and we winged our way back to Point Hope in the golden dusk. That evening as we related our hunting story, Leonard's brothers and their wives fleshed out and cleaned the bear skin. I couldn't believe how quickly the women worked with their sharp half-moon knives, called *ulus*. I also couldn't believe I'd survived my day with combat fuel, the arctic king, and a wild ice pack takeoff. I thrived on adventure, but today's story would last me for awhile. I hoped the rest of the trip would be less harrowing.

March 10 dawned clear and calm, with indications of another beautiful arctic day. We couldn't have asked for better weather on this trip, and I knew it was unusual to have so many successively good flying days. I expected the weather to hold, so instead of immediately returning for the bear meat on the ice pack, I stayed in the village to participate in a yearly custom. In preparation for the whaling season, the Eskimos held a whaling feast.

At mid-forenoon, about 15 villagers gathered at one edge of the village over a large underground cache. My movie camera clicked away as a six-foot whale flipper of one of last year's whales was pulled up. The 300-pound chunk of meat was taken by sled to one of the houses and exposed for thawing in preparation of the next day's feast.

At noon, Leonard and I back-tracked to the ice pack to retrieve the meat—and the gas can. "Doc, it's got to be here some place," said Leonard.

Searching the labyrinth of ice packs, we passed right over the bear remains without seeing them. Finally, I started a wide circle, tightening down until we saw the bloody ice. Knowing how wild an ice pack landing could be, I was relieved to make a fairly smooth landing.

The sun shone brilliantly and even though the temperature was zero, the reflection from the pure white snow caused us to toss off our parkas as we shot more pictures among the deep blue columns of pressure ridges. Then, like two boys at play, we jumped over the ice cracks and looked for seal holes, until Leonard warned, "Hear the ice creak? This stuff could move any time. Let's get over to where the plane is."

We pulled out the emergency gear in the plane and piled in the bear meat. Leonard stayed on the ice as I returned to the village and unloaded. As I shuttled back for Leonard, his brother's families prepared a feast of bear tongue and neck meat for us. Reluctantly, we packed the plane and left the awesome, but treacherous and unforgiving ice.

We'd planned to wash the bear skin in one of the beach water holes that evening, but when we walked to Leonard's brother's house, we found that his father, Mr. Jacob Lane, had already finished the washing and the skin was stretched across tall whale bones to dry.

Dismal overcast and a 15 to 20 mph wind opened on our day March 11. Just as Leonard had predicted, the ice pack had moved out during the night. Even with the foul weather around us, instead of trying to get ahead of the storm, we stayed in the village for the whale feast. The whale was cut into small portions and divided among the people. Leonard offered me some muktuk, the outer layer of the whale, but I had difficulty tolerating the odor, let alone getting it anywhere near my mouth.

During the feast, I had the priviledge of seeing our adopted daughter, Mishal's, natural grandmother, Beatrice Tooyak. I didn't tell her that her curly-haired, energy-plus granddaughter now lived with us, but I did capture her on my movie film so someday I could introduce her to Mishal.

Around noon, we bade farewell to the kind villagers, thanking them for their hospitality and fuel. We left most of the meat with Leonard's family and since the bearskin was now clean and dry, we managed to fit everything—including ourselves—back into the plane without being overloaded. Little did we know what lie ahead as we gassed and packed our plane.

Our course had followed the coastline and we climbed to 2,000 feet to cross over Cape Thompson. That's when the trouble began and the downdrafts threatened to destroy our fragile craft. Now we sat in the darkness, wondering what would happen next and hoping there would be a sequel to this adventure story.

After a fitful night of intermittent sleep, we awoke to find that the wind had shifted to the opposite direction and a gentle ocean breeze now brushed over the enormous drifts, which partially covered the plane's tail and immobilized the plane. We urged our constricted bodies out of their paralzyed positions and nearly fell out of the plane into the deep snow. The end four feet of the fuselage was filled and packed with snow. The only way to clean out this dangerous dead weight was to stick our bare hands through the inspection plate holes. When our hour's work was completed, our hands were frozen. By noon, the ceiling had lifted sufficiently, that we could take off; however, before we could even start the plane, we had to tug it out of the white mire.

Finally, we managed to get off our drifted runway and fly to Kivalina, which was only ten miles away. The weather taunted us again, and heavy snow forced us to stay at this village. As before, the schoolteachers, this time Mr. and Mrs. Bingham, graciously extended their hospitality. After spending the previous night cramped into the plane, we rated their modest accomodations as five-star.

By the morning of March 13, the snow had subsided and we eagerly anticipated getting home that day. Much to our dismay, we butted a 30 to 40 mph headwind toward Kotzebue. It took us two hours and fifteen minutes to cover the mere 85 miles. Without wasting any time, we refueled, checked the weather, and struck out towards Galena. Eventually, the wind decreased as we flew over the white flat tundra toward our next checkpoint, Selawik. Just as on the start of our trip, we had to search for the scattered grove of trees that identified this isolated village.

"Leonard, I think we can still make it in tonight," I said optimistically, as we flew southeast with a benign crosswind. I'd spoken too soon. At the first ridge of low mountains, incredible headwinds of 80 mph attacked us with the dual opposition of dangerous downdrafts. "Hang on!" I shouted, trying to keep the plane under control.

After beating the gale winds for nearly half an hour and seeing the same terrain below me, except from varying altitudes, I decided to fly northeast in a crosswind to alleviate the stress of the windy beating on the plane—and on ourselves. For awhile, this new tack seemed to be satisfactory. "Doc, do you know where we're at?" inquired Leonard, as darkness caught us off guard.

"I'm not sure," I said. "I haven't seen any checkpoints for quite some time."

"We'll need to land sometime soon," he continued. "What's your plan?"

Using the Common Sense approach, we followed a tributary to a fairly large river. It was 6:45 P.M.; the gas gauge had ceased its merry movement; and the river was outlined in darkness. This "landing strip" looked long and wide, but still as I brought the plane down, I was wary about my actual distance from the surface, and about obscured pressure ridges. After all the trouble we'd run into, I got a break. This was the softest landing I'd ever experienced, and since the air blended with the snow, I never knew when we first touched down.

We climbed out of the plane and fell into hip-deep snow. "I guess we'll need our snowshoes," observed Leonard.

Before darkness completely shut us in, we tramped out a runway and found firewood. The roaring fire warmed us one side at a time, as it did the Spam in our skillet. It was funny how simple food tasted so good in rugged conditions such as these.

"I thought you said we'd get "in" tonight," said Leonard, patting me on the arm and laughing. "I didn't know you meant 'into' the plane."

At least we didn't have wind battering us as we climbed into our cocoons and prepared for another night out—or "in," as it was in our case.

It wasn't hard to get up early after spending a night squashed in the plane. We flew down the river, and twenty miles later we unexpectedly came upon Koyukuk, where we were able to refuel what seemed to be our always empty gas tank. Now that we knew where we were and the weather decided to stop beating at us, we were able to find our way to Galena and then back to Tanana.

In addition to numerous stories, some of which would be later verified by my movie pictures, I bestowed upon my family some bear meat and souvenirs. Ruby, who would try anything once, reluctanty prepared large bear steaks. The odor forced us to generously allow Leonard to give the rest of the meat to an Eskimo family in the village. I could understand why Ruby preferred the Eskimo sunglasses made from shiny caribou hooves, a whale bone ceremonial mask, and black-and-white ivory watchband.

A week later, Leonard walked into my hospital office with a newspaper in his hand. "Hey, Doc, you made the news." He pointed to a short article, which read:

> Thursday, March 20, 1958
> 64 POLAR BEARS KILLED, ARCTIC
> 34 FOR TROPHIES
> A total of 64 polar bear were
> taken since January in the Arctic,
> according to Stanley Frederickson,
> U.S. Fish and Wildlife Agent, who
> with Sig Olson, Wildlife Manager,
> returned this week from a tour of
> the Arctic Coast area. Of the 64,
> Eskimos took 30 and trophy hunters
> 34. Of the latter, three were
> taken by dog teams out of Point

Hope, but most by plane off the
three-mile limit.

It looked as though I'd gotten in with the action-which is certainly what I enjoyed. I couldn't wait to get back my movies: there would be proof of the action.

11
Break-up takeoff
April 1958

Lights. Action. I wiped off my camera lens.

People congregated in clumps along the steep banks of the Yukon, nudging one another, laughing, and even placing bets on the anticipated action. Children threw rocks and sticks down the bank, aiming for a pop bottle.

Even though ducks and geese were returning north to announce springtime and on this particular spring day the temperature had soared to 50 degrees, something more was drawing young and old out of hibernation.

Let me digress to mention what the main attraction on this April morning was not. One might have assumed it was the annual river breakup, for the riverbank lineup was the same, but that was yet to come. For cheechakos, sourdoughs, and Natives alike, the thundering Yukon breakup was something no one ever quite got used to. No, sir, each year there were bets placed on the day and time it would take place. It could happen anytime in April or May. A year ago, it had moved out of Fairbanks on April 18, passed Nenana on April 28, and then finally shoved through Tanana on May 16.

When the river breakup actually took place, the entire village was notified. Sometimes, someone would run to the Episcopal church to announce the event by ringing the bell. Last year, it surprised us at 3:30 a.m. and I asked the nurse on duty to blow the fire whistle. When notification came at night, people scurried out of their houses for a "come-as-you-are" riverbank party in bathrobes, nightgowns, and stocking feet. If it was daytime, school was dismissed for a real-life science exhibit. At the hospital, nurses and even some patients ran out the door to join the celebration.

Ruby described the massive event in a letter to her parents:

> Yesterday, the ice started to move in one large mass at 3:30 A.M., Can you imagine a mass a half mile wide and a half mile long moving at once? It is a thrilling wonder! After a half hour, the ice jammed and then this morning at 6:00 A.M., it started again and the large mass moved forward. For the next couple days we can expect mammoth ice cubes, all cramming together and floating together, covering the entire surface of the river.

In anticipation, the natives watched the river for signs of breakup—the rotten ice in the middle of the river and freed anchor ice along the edges of the river. When these condition were there, the village men would return from trapping wolverines, red fox, rabbits, beavers, and wolves.

In the fall, anchor ice was the first to freeze. In spring it was the first to break loose. Just the week before, the anchor ice had popped loose and now the villagers were preparing for a new fishing season by repairing fishing wheels, fishing traps, and drying racks.

The anchor ice extended downward into the riverbed, forming a solid mass approximately four to six feet thick. Reaching toward the center of the river, it would catch floating river ice chunks, anchoring them until the entire ice flow would freeze in place.

During the winter, the water flowing beneath the ice decreased, shrinking into the riverbed ten to twenty feet away from the shore and the anchor ice. Then in spring, the melting snow would increase the flow, causing the river not only to fill its original bed, but to overflow, cover the anchor ice, until bouyed up by the pressure it would snap loose. The broken anchor ice would then float downstream a short distance before jamming together with unbroken anchor ice. Subsequently, there were sections along the river with muddy channels of water ten to twenty feet wide between the shore and the main ice.

Not only did breakup signal fishing time, it also meant time to catch winter firewood. Reluctantly dragged away by the mighty Yukon, the ice clawed at the banks, desperately seeking a firm grasp, but instead found and tore away tottering, root-exposed trees. After the ice had majestically thrashed and ploughed down the river, it lost itself in the slate-gray Bering Sea.

In its wake, the toppled trees and sandbar driftwood gaily paraded down the river. The Natives joined the parade, racing around in their kicker boats, dodging the debris, snagging firewood, and then towing their catch back to shore to dry out. Cutting and stacking came later.

But now back to my story. This breakup had not happened, yet all eyes were riveted to the river's edge, across from the hospital. There sandwiched on the shore between the steep 15-foot bank and the open channel of water, which was approximately 40 feet wide and several hundred feet long, crouched a Super Cub—on skis. This plane was the subject of speculation. Word had gotten around that this morning the pilot planned to takeoff from the barely 50-foot mixture of crushed ice and honey-combed snow. "Would the plane crack-up on the shore, or end up in the water?" People were asking.

What I was wondering was why the plane was still there? A month earlier, I'd moved my plane away from the anchor ice, off the river, and onto the runway outside the village. Somehow, like a misplaced snow goose missing its cue to migrate south, this plane had missed its cue to leave while the strong, wide river ice provided a long, sturdy airstrip.

It wasn't as though the plane had not received advance warning of its disappearing security. Two weeks ago, Wally, my lab technician, who had come to Alaska from the Eastern Seaboard, had curiously set off across the half-mile Yukon River ice. Wally was not adept at reading the tell-tale sign of impending breakup: that of rotten ice. He did not realize that the sun melted the surface ice, while the swift current, with similar intent, eroded the ice from beneath. To a newcomer, the resulting one-foot crystalized "candle ice" looked trustworthy, when in fact, it could not consistently sustain a man's weight.

Unaware of the danger, Wally had confidently trudged through the worn-out snow on the river and around the winter-aged pressure heaves. He, like me, used all his moments off work to explore the wonders of this fascinating frontier. The sun had smiled brightly as he had leaned against a slanted ice wall to rest at midpoint. Suddenly, his peaceful world exploded and his feet had dropped beneath him! Frantically, he had struggled in the paralyzing water. With no moments to spare, he flailed his arms above the ice, grasped a firm chunk of ice, and dragged himself out of the frigid blackness. A wiser Wally beat a fast retreat back to shore; well, as fast as an adrenaline-powered man can cautiously crawl. His experience was a lesson for me: nature's clues needed to be learned and heeded.

"Here they come," yelled one of the bystanders. The children stopped throwing rocks down the bank, and there was a momentary lull in conversation. Out of the hospital walked a man confidently swinging a suitcase followed by a woman carrying a baby. Down the gravel incline they marched toward the plane.

Who would be so foolhardy as to attempt flying off the token airstrip—much less, endangering two other people? I knew the man and the plane. It was none other then Don Stickman. Don, a bush pilot, was a living legend—at least to this point in time he was living. I wasn't sure of his past, but I'd heard that he had served in the Air Force and had thousands of flying hours to his credit. The middle-aged Indian had a reputation of being able to fly in any weather, at any time, under any circumstances. Ice fog, blizzard, total darkness. 30–40° below zero. But, could he get his plane with skis out of this predicament?

Don lived downriver, but his escapades would either travel upriver through my patients or filter into the hospital whenever Don happened to be in the village. For instance, one day a patient asked me, "Say, Doc, you know what Don is up to now? Wolf hunting."

Bounty hunting could provide a substantial means of income for some Natives—without endangering the species. Most of the world's wolf population resided in Alaska, Canada, and the Soviet Union, with an estimated 5,200 to 6,500 in Alaska. Bounty hunting and trapping only approached 15 percent of the wolf population.

My patient went on to describe Don's hunting strategy. He flew low over the treetops, spotted the wolf, and then flushed it out into the open. His backseat "gunner" leaned out the open door as Don rolled the plane over for a clear shot. After landing and retrieving their bounty, Don again searched for a wolf, while at the same time checking his controls, watching for a place to land, and hopefully staying above the treetops.

That winter, Don scored 125 wolves, which sold for $50 bounty each, plus the sale of their pelts. Good money. Tricky flying.

"Doc, have you seen Don's plane?" asked Wally one afternoon. Between patients, we slipped out the hospital's backdoor. It seemed appropriate that Don's plane convalesced below the riverbank in front of the hospital. Tape and bailing wire bandaged the engine and injured tail.

Now Don was preparing for another adventure; and I was concerned about whether or not this one could have a happily-ever-after ending since his passengers were my patients. Ten days ago, Doris had delivered a healthy baby girl. Yesterday she told me, "Dr. Gaede, I want to go back home now."

"How will you get back to your village?" I asked.

"I think Don Stickman is in the village," she replied.

"Yes, he has been here about two weeks now." I said. "But forget his help. There is no way he can take off from where he's parked."

"Dr. Gaede, I know he's on the beach," she smiled reassuringly, her black braids bobbing up and down as she nodded her head. "Really, Dr. Gaede. I'll be o.k. with Don."

I felt responsible for Doris, and my concern for her safety outweighed the thrill of capturing this event on film. I handed my movie camera to Wally, who had slipped up beside me, and scrambled down the bank to Don.

"Don, how are you going to take off?"

"Don't worry, Doc, I've done this before," he grinned.

"Don, the gravel will tear up your skis, plus you have two other people . . ."

"Hey, Doc, just watch." Seeing the determination on his

face, I realized that there was as much chance of changing his mind as that of a spawning salmon swimming upstream.

A cloud darkened the sky as I surveyed the situation. The plane's skis rested on the disappearing snow, Doris cooed to her just awakened baby; and Don casually leaned against one of the plane's struts. The characters of this adventure plot seemed oblivious to the nearby murky stream of water and the crushed river ice. As I reluctantly returned to my filming position, I consoled myself that most of the hospital personnel were literally on stand-by in case of an emergency.

"Doc, what did he say?"

"Do you think he can do it?"

"Boy, I'm glad I'm not his passenger."

Questions multiplied as the people voiced their apprehension.

I narrowed in on the plane through my camera lens. Don pulled the plane to the edge of his runway to gain the greatest length possible for takeoff. Doris climbed in. Don handed her the baby and suitcase. Then he slowly walked around the plane, touching a spot here and there, moving the flaps, turning the prop, then crawling in. The engine easily started. Riverbank chatter stopped.

"Boy, that's a short strip," I said to no one in particular.

"And the water's cold," added Wally, knowingly.

After a brief warmup, the plane roared across the snow. Quickly it devoured the snow patch and deliberately edged over to the water trough. Don was going to water ski! Could the 15 to 20 mph groundspeed hold him above the water? Was the water runway long enough? Would he get enough lift before smashing into the jammed anchor ice a short distance down the river?

Powerfully, the plane skied onto the water, leaving a wide wake. Incredible! The skis supported the plane's weight until gracefully it lifted off, becoming a dark silhouette against the pale Alaskan sky. As the sun shone warmly and the ice continued to melt, the crowd clapped, then slowly dispersed, back to fishing repairs, the general store, the hospital, and the CAA housing compound.

After everyone was gone, I stood and looked over the empty gray and white set. The only remaining signs of the edge-of-your-seat thriller were double ski tracks slashed through the disintegrating ice patch and a widening wake of gray waves gently lapping against the gravel shore.

Once again, I was a believer. Don could fly anywhere, in anything, at anytime. And, if anyone was to question me about the truth of Don's stories, I had film to show them the facts. What a plot. What an action line. What a set. Tanana might have lacked TVs and stage plays, but it didn't lack the stuff movies and drama were made of.

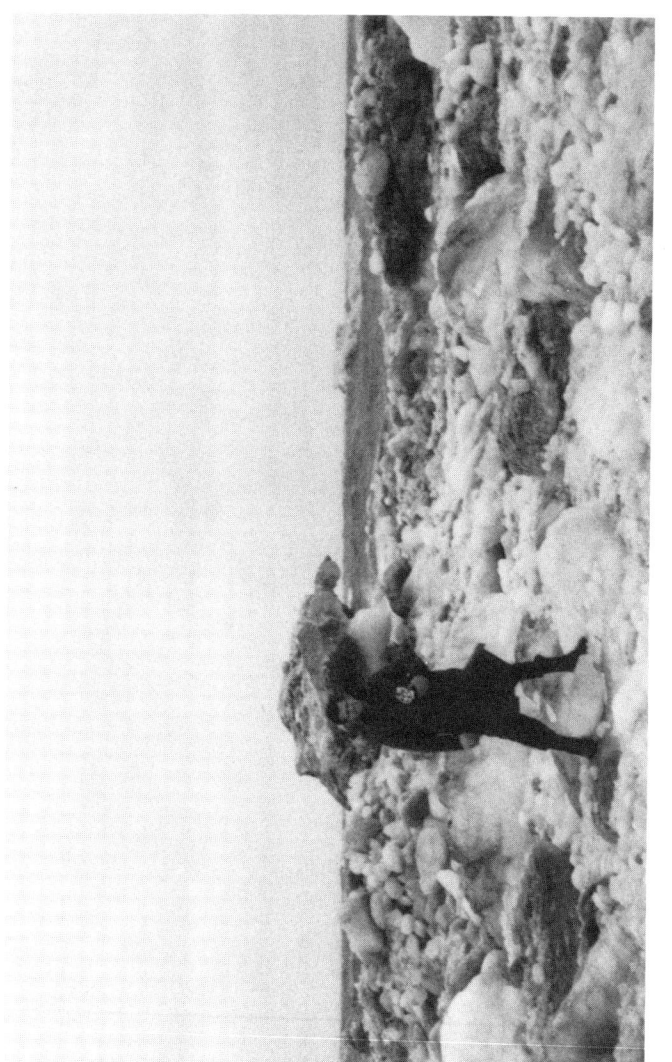

On Barrow's icy beach - July, 1959.

Presbyterian Church at Barrow - July, 1959.

Endless lakes near Barrow - July, 1959.

Eskimo woman at Anaktuvuk Pass - April, 1959.

Missionaries at Ruby.

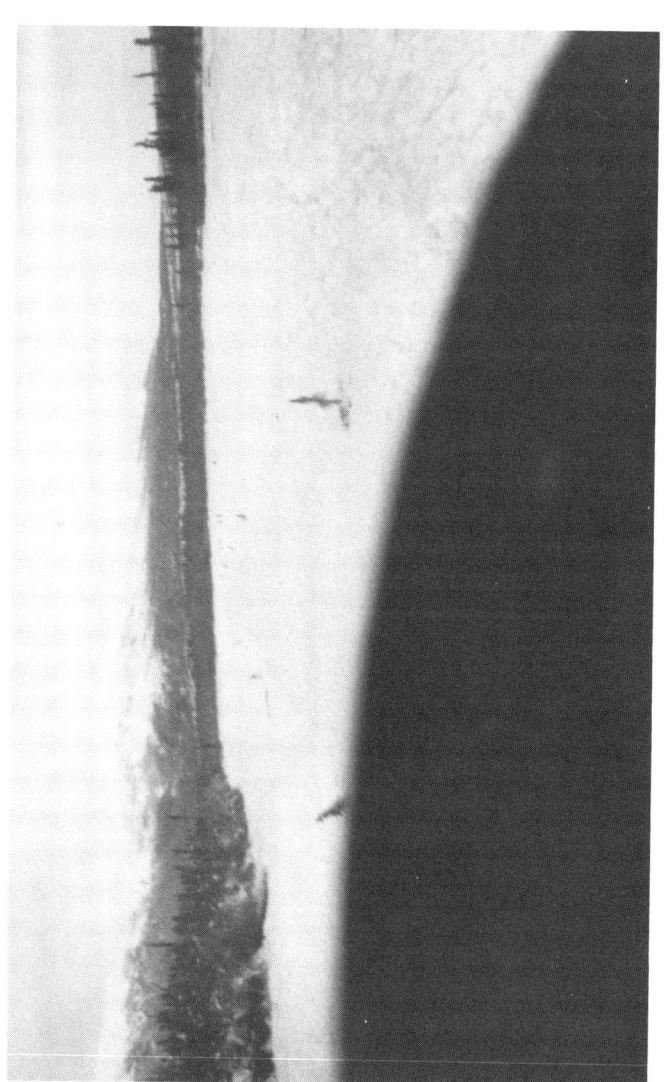

Landing on marked runway on Stony River - November, 1956.

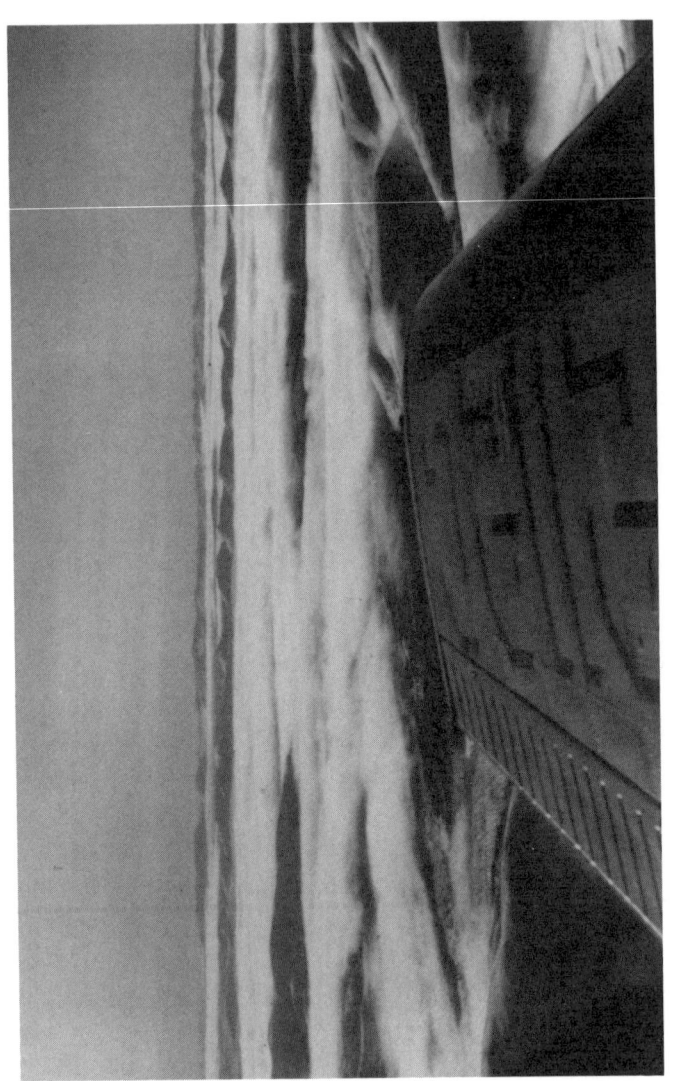

Ice fog near Sparvon - January, 1957.

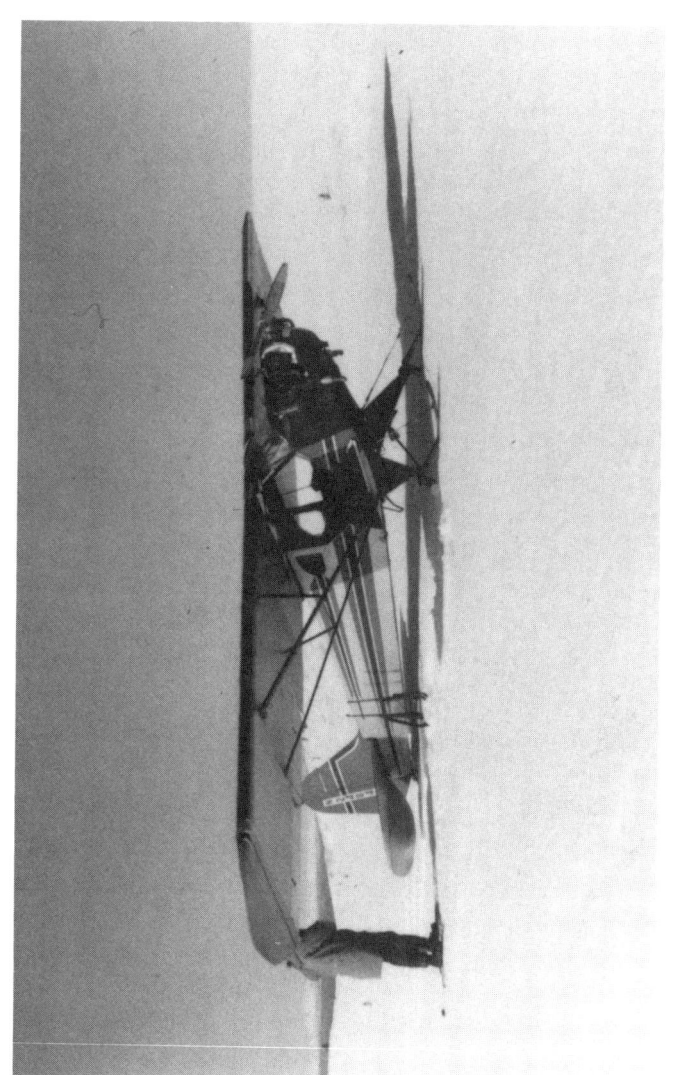

Plane on ridge of Talkeetna mountain - April, 1957.

Community Hall at Tanana - July, 1957.

Christmas pot lache.

Dog sled races on Yukon - April, 1958.

Tanana School - March, 1957.

Kaltag caches - April, 1958.

Our landing field on sheep hunt in Brooks Range - September, 1958.

Ruby and her moose - September, 1958.

Taxiing on Boney Creek - July, 1958.

Point Hope graveyard.

Fishing at Brooks River Falls - June, 1957.

Emergency shelter (sod house) on Arctic beach - July, 1959.

12
Hunting: Not for men only
September 1958

It was that time of year when the early morning frost beckoned the golden leaves from the birch trees and the geese headed south. Crisp air pulled away the sunshine's warmth and a wool jacket felt more comfortable than scratchy. It was moose-hunting season. On this particular year, the moose appeared plentifully along the Yukon River, and we were allowed to hunt the same day that we flew.

"Ruby, this is not for men only," I cajoled my wife. "You're a rugged Alaskan woman and a strong-stomached farm girl." I thought this was a fair statement even though she was only 5 foot 2 inches tall. And it was true in the sense that she was familiar with guns and hunting.

"I really don't have time, and I certainly don't want to stay out overnight," she countered.

"I'll just take you down the Yukon a few miles, spot your moose, land on a sandbar, you shoot your moose, and we'll return by dark," I explained. "You know how easily I helped those two Natives get their moose just last week."

"I just don't know," she said. "Who will watch the children?"

"One of the nurses or schoolteachers could," I suggested.

"I just don't know," she said again. "The weather has been overcast . . . and you know how I feel about landing on the beach, and . . ."

"Now Ruby, you know I no longer have a puddle-jumper. My new plane is nearly first-class."

Our growing family could not fit into the J-3, so I'd sold it for a four-place PA 14 Family Cruiser. Parting with the J-3 wasn't easy. When Mark had watched the Christmas-tree-colored J-3 take off from the river without me, he'd cried, "That's my plane, it's a nice plane, too." I remembered the first time I'd taken him up in it, and he'd sat as quiet as a mouse on Ruby's lap. Ruth, who seldom let her excitement show, reflected the opposite emotions when I'd flown the new plane in from Fairbanks and parked it on the airstrip. She'd actually jumped up and down all around the plane, patting its red finish. I was elated, too, with the luxuries: an inside starter so no longer would I have to hand-prop my plane; A radio to hear weather reports en route or call for help; landing lights.

In spite of all these upgrades, I still shared Mark's sad feelings. As I stood on the banks of the Yukon, watching that small plane with large memories become a speck in the broad Alaskan sky, I felt especially nostalgic, remembering my experiences with it on floats. For example, the plane was a great fisherman's friend. Not only that, it seemed that it was also a great story-maker.

Take that Saturday in August, when I'd walked over to Arctic Missions missionary, Mel Jenson's, to inquire about fishing. "Mel, where's a good spot for catching shee fish?"

"Let's try the Tozi River," he suggested. "It's only eleven miles down the river."

We flew down the Yukon and in a few minutes landed at the mouth of the Tozi. I carefully edged the floats over to a coarse gravel beach and docked. We stepped off the floats in our hip boots, into the shallow water, and toward the hollowed-out

Hunting: Not for men only

bank, where we cast off with our daredevil lures. It wasn't long before we had not only a string of shee fish, but northern pike as well. "This ought to take care of a few meals," said Mel, as he hopped onto the float and swung his long legs into the plane.

I pushed the plane off the sandbar and jumped onto the right float as we drifted out into the 6 to 8 mph river current. While standing on the float, I hand-propped the plane. Immediately, the engine fired and I climbed into my seat. Run up seemed normal, so I pushed the throttle open and prepared to take off. That's when I noticed something was wrong.

The plane seemed glued to the water. Acceleration was very sluggish, and the plane did not come up on the "step." Curiously, I looked out the right window. A-o.k. I checked out the left window. Where was my left float? There it hung a half-inch below the water. Naturally, I aborted takeoff and returned to the shore, making a preliminary diagnosis of a hole in the float.

We dragged the plane as far out of the water as was possible and started our investigation. "Here's the problem, Mel," I said. "The middle compartment in the float is nearly filled with water. We must have thirty to forty gallons in there."

In a half hour, I'd pumped out the water and located the offender, a quarter-sized ragged hole in the thin aluminum near the center.

"Do you have any ideas for improvising a patch?" I asked, as I rummaged through my meager emergency gear.

"I'll show you a bush technique for boat or float emergency repair," he answered, walking off along the shore.

A few minutes later he returned with a cutoff half-inch alder branch. I watched him without asking questions as from the inside of the float compartment he first packed his blue hankerchief into the hole, cut the branch, then placed it against the hanky. Pressure held it in place as it wedged tightly against the opposite side of the float. "This should get us home," he said as he closed the float cover.

Once again, I taxied out into the river. Both floats rode normally and I expected to be home within minutes.

Wrong. As soon as I'd taken off, the throttle went wild. The engine uncontrollably wound up to full throttle. I managed to circle the river, switch off the engine, and plop down on the river. With my emergency paddle I manuveured the plane to shore and a second time made an emergency inspection.

This time, the throttle cable had broken, leaving me without power control. Upon finding some wire in my emergency gear, I jury-rigged the fuel control with two wires: one to open the throttle, and the other to close it. I threaded the wire from the carburetor into the cabin through the outside of the cowling and door edge.

"Mel, ready for Take Three?" I asked, taxiing back out into the river.

Well, that was only one of the many experiences with the J-3, and I hoped that now with the Family Cruiser I'd make new memories, all with happy endings. Returning to my task at hand, I continued my points of persuasion. "Ruby, I even have tundra tires. They are big and durable so that we can safely land on nearly anything."

"O.k. o.k." she finally consented. "I'll try anything once."

And so, the chain of events began as I predicted. One evening, Anna Bortel, one of the schoolteachers, stayed with the children as we flew fifteen miles down the Yukon. "Look Ruby, there he is!" I said excitedly, pointing to a moose bedded down in a dried swamp on an island less than 200 yards from the river. Sunlight flashed off his large 65- to 70-inch rack as he turned his head.

We landed on a wet, slightly soft sandbar about 600 feet long. The moose waited for us in deep grass and autumn red bushes just beyond a thick grove of spruce trees between the swamp and our sand bar. This would be easy. I put on my backpack and carried my 300 H & H. Softly we crashed through the incredibly dense underbrush, over large, flat, moldy-looking mushrooms and around velvety, moss-covered stumps. In the tree's shadows, light snow dusted low-lying flaming red cranberry bushes. Tightly gnarled alders held us back and five-foot-tall grass obscured our view.

"What about bear?" Ruby whispered apprehensively. "You've told me they're in tall grass like this."

"Don't worry," I said, as we broke onto a narrow trail, which I hoped wasn't a bear trail. I kept my ears trained for the sound of their warning "woof."

After about fifteen minutes, I cautioned her to be silent, since any moment we would come out into the yellow swamp and see her giant bull moose. Slowly the woods parted and we looked around.

"This somehow looks familiar," said Ruby.

And then I saw it. I couldn't believe my eyes. There in front of us was the plane. We'd walked in a complete circle, pulling toward the right, which was a very common error in overcast or evening skies.

"I made a slight miscalculation," I stammered. "Let's try it again."

"Not tonight," she said. "I am *not* going back in there again. I want to go home."

The light rain was on her side, so we headed back to the plane. As we walked, I observed the shore and how our feet squished into the fine sand. Even with tundra tires, the drag would increase the necessary distance for takeoff. In addition, the 115 hp engine was underpowered for this kind of strip.

I tried to appear nonchalant as we climbed in and I said to Ruby, "Hold the flashlight so I can see the speed indicator. When we hit 45 let me know and I'll pull off." I hated to include her in this bush takeoff, since I knew it would do nothing to build her confidence for a return hunt.

The plane rolled along the sticky sand and sluggishly gathered speed. "45!" I used first notch of flaps and pulled back on the stick. The plane lifted off, but hovered over the water barely above stall speed. At treetop level, I retracted my flaps. I would have to get a bigger engine before trying a stunt like this again—or I would lose all my passengers from fear. Ruby never said a word and immediately upon landing in Tanana, she very tightly lipped climbed out of the plane and walked home silently.

I don't know what made me do it, but several weeks later, I actually heard myself saying to Ruby as she had her back to me washing breakfast dishes, "Ruby, what about another try at moose hunting?" Still blundering along, I continued, "There's a bull with his harem just a couple of miles up-river. In fact, it's so close to home that we can be there in a few minutes."

She didn't say a word. She scrubbed the same dish over and over. Silence. Deciding that this was a lost cause, I turned to leave. "Elmer, you know how I feel about your flying," she stopped me with her slow words. "And I don't know much about hunting . . . but if you *promise* . . . not to take any chances again, I'll go."

Excitedly, I made the rounds at the hospital and contacted Mrs. Neufeld, one of the nurses, to see if she could stay with Mark and Mishal, since Naomi and Ruth were in school. At noon, I threw the hunting gear into the plane, the 300 H & H for myself, and an 8 mm Mauser for Ruby.

We took off toward the confluence of the Yukon and Tanana rivers. Just as I thought, the moose I had previously spotted were still feeding in a narrow meadow just off the side of the Tanana River. The bull lay surrounded by his three fair ladies.

"How does he look to you?" I asked Ruby, pointing out his distinguished masculine broad rack.

"He looks like meat for our table," she remarked, not too enthusiastically.

"O.k. let's go after him," I said cheerfully, trying to buoy her attitude.

I searched for a place to land and found a 60-foot wide empty slough about a quarter mile from the moose. Although the dark sand indicated wetness, I decided that my tundra tires could land without a problem. I didn't want to spook the moose, so I pulled full flaps and glided quietly onto the sand. The plane rolled for about 150 feet, then abruptly stopped. Ruby climbed out of the plane and immediately sank a couple inches into the sand. At the same time, we both saw water filling up the tire tracks. Things were not starting well.

We walked over to the small stream of water separating us from the moose, and much to our dismay found it to be too deep to cross. "Don't worry, we will find your moose someplace else," I said, remaining optimistic.

Together, we pushed the plane out of the gray muck, and I taxied the plane up to firmer ground where we took off and flew downriver 35 miles. There along a beautiful, firm shore stood a moose. "This could be it, Ruby," I said over my shoulder. I dropped down to see if it had a rack, and sure enough he had some short spikes. I landed on the smooth sand and we both jumped out with our guns. The moose started to run and in the excitement I forgot that it was Ruby's moose and shot, but didn't know if I had hit it. He splashed into the stream and then crashed off into the woods. I didn't like to leave a possibly wounded animal, so we hiked after him, but soon realized that it would do us no good in the thick underbrush and tall trees. Even when we took off and flew low over the area, we could not find it.

It was now 3:30 P.M. and as we headed home, I decided to check if the other bull had remained in the meadow with his pleasant companions. Just as I suspected, he was there. This time, I thought more carefully about my landing strip and found a dryer area—which was on the same side as the moose. In like fashion, before heading into the woods, I checked my compass and scrutinized every landmark. I couldn't afford to make the same embarrassing mistake as on the initial hunt; otherwise, this would be Ruby's final hunt.

Through the woods we hiked. I didn't know how the wild animals managed to keep track of themselves, as we climbed over fallen timber, around mini bogs, and through tall grass. The towering spruce trees refused to let the sun in, and on several occasions, as we stumbled into a faded brown swamps with spindly swamp spruce, we were surprised by the sudden brightness. Ruby bravely trudged along, apparently suppressing her fears of bears and being lost.

"I think they're just ahead," I whispered to Ruby. We edged forward, hugging the brush. I peered around the meadow. Nothing. "I'll try calling him." I pulled out a piece of moose rack and raked it across a nearby birch tree. We crouched in silence. After a moment, we heard the bull return the call by rubbing his rack on a tree.

"I hope he doesn't charge," said Ruby.

We crept closer. I could smell him. Then there he was lumbering toward us. His huge head and broad lowered rack moving steadily. I didn't know if he was there to challenge us or to protect his female interests, I just knew he was enormous. I backed up, bumping into Ruby. "Get ready!"

The moose picked up speed. Ruby froze. "Shoot, Ruby! Shoot!" I yelled. She stood paralyzed in his path. By now he was too close for comfort. Frantically, I focused my gun on the monster and as I pulled the trigger, I heard another shot ring out. Only 37 yards away from us, the moose crashed to the ground. I didn't know which was shaking harder, the ground from the impact, or Ruby as she turned to me with terrified eyes.

"You did great," I softly encouraged her. "Now finish him off." She managed to lift the gun and with two shots stilled the quivering giant. Our hearts continued to quiver as the previous minutes replayed themselves in our minds.

Already this season, I'd gutted three other moose, so I immediately went to work undressing the 900-pound hunk of meat. Ruby had never seen this stage of moose-hunting, although she had cut up and packaged pounds of meat after they had been packed home. She appeared to have recovered her sense of speech as she commented nonstop about the the innards of the moose. "He's like a camel," she said. "Just look at all that blood and liquid. And look at his heart—the size of my head."

"At least he can cool down overnight, and then Roy Gronning and I will skin him and pack out the meat tomorrow morning," I said, since the evening darkness hurried us away from her trophy. I decided to take a short cut back, and as a precaution against getting lost, we marked a toilet paper trail. After my blunder on the first hunt, I was glad to see the plane—and not the meadow or any circled toilet paper.

Getting Ruby's moose was not over. Roy and I did go back and bring back the meat, followed by a another trip by Leonard Lane and myself in which we skinned out the head in order to have the head mounted with rack. Since I didn't have my movie camera along to record this story, I figured that in this way, Ruby would have proof of her successful wild game hunt—and that she could bring home the moose and cook it, too.

13
Close encounters of many kinds
October 1958

"Doc! What's your stall speed?" yelled Pete.

I pulled my gaze up from searching for white critters, and I looked down. My airspeed had dropped to 44 mph—almost stall speed—and I was about to nest in the treetops. Immediately I applied full throttle, pushed the stick forward, and barely cleared the trees.

Pete, the hospital maintenance supervisor, had joined me this morning as I'd pointed the Family Cruiser north toward the Ray Mountains.

From the air, clumps of yellow and yellow-orange birch dotted the variagated green spruce, letting us know the all-too-short Alaskan summer was coming to an end. We flew over

Allakaket, positioned on the Koyukok River, up the Alatna River, and into the Brooks Range. Low-lying purple-red berry bushes now replaced the golden birch, and the pale gray granite gave the illusion of snow on the mountainsides. In other areas, the real snow reached down toward timberline. Swirls of clouds decorated the sky above the picture-perfect landscape below.

Following the river into this seldom-hunted area, we spotted dozens of moose, their antlers reflecting the sun as they ate breakfast in the meadows. An occasional black bear splashed in the river to check out breakfast possibilities. Soon we spotted the white we thought we were looking for. A close fly-by along a sheer mountain ledge turned the specks into a herd of about twenty sheep.

Neither of us had ever hunted sheep before. "I imagine there must be a legal ram somewhere in that herd," I told Pete. Suffering from a kind of amnesia about my other hunts, I was optimistic about this hunt. All we had to do was land, hike over to the sheep, find the ram and return home successful hunters—all in a day's work.

The Alatna had no suitable sandbars on the mountain side of the river, so we looked for an alternate landing area. One potential landing strip appeared to be an old dry riverbed. To get a closer view, I used first-notch flaps, slowed the plane down to 55 mph, and skimmed the trees. Not realizing the deceiving rise in the elevation of the riverbed, I slowly pulled back the stick to near stall speed. I'd been too busy to notice my predicament until Pete yelled at me about the stall speed.

After several more passes, I was confident that the riverbed, with scattered 2-foot aspen and spruce, would make a fairly smooth 800-foot landing strip. We could dodge the small trees and my durable tundra tires would take care of the rest. I lowered the flaps, passed over a large bull moose, and committed for landing. Too late I realized my error. I had misjudged the height of the "small" trees, which were now growing up to 10 and 12 feet. There was nothing we could do now but brace ourselves and hope for the best.

Like the threshing machines I'd grown up with in Kansas, the plane threshed the leaves from the trees, then came to an abrupt stop as the leading edge encountered a large "small" tree. Amazingly enough, we and the plane were still intact.

Pete and I climbed out to survey this environment that had ensnared us. "I think we just initiated your new plane," said Pete, eyeing the gold-green aspen leaves adorning the red struts. We walked along the "smooth" riverbed, which was gravel-packed and uneven. Unlike the rising trees, the 800-foot airstrip had shrunk. At the most, it was 300 feet of "axe and shovel work," and after that it suddenly fell off into a 12-foot gully.

"Let's worry about this later," I suggested to Pete, after working for awhile to clear the airstrip. "We came here to hunt, so let's get going."

With my 8mm Mouser and Pete's 3.06, we started our ascent. A game trail made the hike easier, but brought with it another encounter: a full-grown black bear. Plump in preparation for hibernation, he lazily waddled straight for us with no indication of stopping. We banged our packboards and shouted. I knew that black bear had poor eyesight, but this one seemed to be unusually hard of hearing, as well. As if he had definite plans, he swayed along toward us on a collision course. We clamored about trying to untangle our guns when finally, at 100 feet, he snorted and slowly veered off the path and ambled around us.

"That was too close!" I said to Pete, hearing my voice shake.

We continued winding up the mountainside, over a broad section of slippery shale, and onto a grassy mountain bench, where we had spotted the sheep from the air. We looked around. No sheep. Cautiously, we hiked another quarter-mile.

"Maybe the sheep have spooked into the crags," offered Pete. "Let's look over the edge."

We crawled to the edge of the bench and peered down. Only more ledges of gray rock. No white sheep. "They have to be here someplace. Let's just sit quietly and wait," I recommended. They were certainly at an advantage since we did not have the freedom to climb where they could. Their gravity-defying safety was our danger.

Thirty minutes slowly crept by as we sat absorbed in the absolute quiet. White clouds grazed on the purple, windswept mountains to our north. Then as I was just leaning over to discuss a new strategy with Pete, we were rewarded by a clatter below, followed by a single-file parade of thirty pure-white animals—most with one-eighth to one-quarter curls.

The several young ones turned their gentle black eyes and serious faces toward us , before nudging their mothers and trying to hurry along the procession.

"Hey, Pete." I whispered. "Where's the ram? Do you see a three-quareter curl? . . . Are you sure these are sheep?"

The great white ram we'd planned to encounter was nowhere in sight. Puzzled, we stood there discussing what to do next. A stiff gust of chilly wind chased down our necks and helped us decide. We headed down the mountain, back to the job of clearing the airstrip.

As we worked, the chill left our bodies and the major obstacles left the takeoff course. At this point, we found ourselves down by the gully. "Doc, how are we going to get out of here now?" Pete questioned. One thing was certain: with the abbreviated airstrip, we would not be able to take off loaded as we had come in.

"Let's empty the plane of gear and ten gallons of gas, and I'll fly solo over to an adjacent sandbar." I answered. Hopefully that "suitable strip" would not be a mirage as had been the riverbed.

To transport Pete and the gear the 50 feet across the river to the sandbar, we lashed together some of the trees we'd chopped down and made a raft. Pete would simply wade with the floating gear through the shallow water.

Only one problem remained: the gully. Remembering hangar advice, I dug a shallow trench and planted a six-inch log firmly in the ground just before the drop-off. Pete asked, "What's that for?"

"Just in case I don't get airborne before I reach the gully, my tundra tires will hit the log and I'll bounce into the air," I explained.

He shook his head, but couldn't come up with a better idea.

We pulled the plane back into the trees as far as possible. Pete held onto the tail as I climbed in, started the engine, and gave it full throttle, using first-notch flaps and holding down the brakes. The engine roared, covering Pete with dust and torn-up leaves.

Released from Pete's grip, the empty plane bounced crazily over the rough gravel and tree stumps. The gully rushed toward me. Just a few feet before hitting the "last chance" log, it became airborne. I wiped the sweat off my forehead and circled for landing.

After successfully letting down on the wide, smooth, 1,200-foot sandbar, I got ready for Pete by building a driftwood campfire. At least my cold-legged partner could warm himself after his walk in the river.

Pete tossed a rope across the river to me and then fastened the other end to our loaded raft. I was sure he would have no trouble fording the river. Slowly he eased himself down the bank and into the water. Then suddenly he slid into the icy water and dropped out of sight. What had happened to Pete? How could this shallow creek swallow him up? Was this, too, an illusion?

Pete, who had once been a lifeguard, bobbed up and grabbed onto the raft to keep it upright as it dipped from side to side. I pulled the rope. Pete howled out about the frigid water. None too soon, the raft and my shivering partner docked at the sandbar. Pete let me deal with the raft as he stripped off his wet clothes and threw himself at the fire's welcome warmth. Between the two of us, we managed to find enough dry clothes in our packs to redress Pete.

It was soon time to decide on our next move. We had used up most of the day. Should we spend the night here? Should we fly back to Tanana? A commotion across the river interrupted our conversation. There before us was a trophy bull moose, checking us out with his nose-filled face. As we stood staring, it plunged into the river and swam toward us. Uneven waves of water spread before him.

"Is this rutting season, Pete?" I said anxiously. "I think we're being challenged." Our sandbar was devoid of trees or any hiding place. I hoped he wasn't like a domestic bull and attracted to red, or my plane would be his target—although I could sacrifice that for my life.

We yelled and pounded our cooking pans together. Shaking its 70-inch rack, the bull continued its approach. We ran for our guns. About 100 feet from us it, like the bear, apparently changed its mind and decided to detour around the two obnoxious creatures on the sandbar.

Enough was enough. Not knowing what else could possibly happen to us in one day, and mindful of light rain coming down from heavy evening clouds, we took off, turning our plane toward Bettles, about 70 miles away. There we could find some safe, indoor camping.

As visibility rapidly deteriorated, we followed the twisting river 200 feet below. In about 30 minutes the Bettle's beacon, like a friendly lighthouse, welcomed us.

Later, comfortably full of moose steak, Pete and I sat in front of a crackling fireplace in a snug, log cabin with FAA* friends, telling and reliving our wild and woolly adventures of the day. The encounters with the tree stumps, gully, bear, and moose were clear in my mind, but I still wondered, what were those white animals we'd seen?

Note
*CAA changed to FAA when Alaska became a state.

14
Tooth-pullin' time
Winter 1959

"Please Dr. Gaede—I'm brave." The somber Indian boy begged me with both his eyes and words. Nearby, a group of his friends flaunted the holes in their mouths, prior habitats for decayed teeth. "I'm tough," the thin, small teenager continued softly.

My anesthetic supplies were depleted and I knew his tooth could wait until my next visit to Kaltag, a small village 200 miles down the Yukon River. At the same time, I was keenly aware that this boy's request had surfaced not out of medical need, but out of a newly assumed social need. As I toyed with the forceps, the silver metal took on a new shape. I was holding in my hands the key to his acceptance. How could he go home, the only boy that evening without the trophy-wound to prove his manhood among his peers? The boy's request had prompted laughter in the crowded schoolroom-turned-office where a baby cried, two preschoolers played tag with a husky pup, and several of the older men chronically coughed. Then there was silence as 20 to 30 villagers listened for my reply. I felt caught in the middle holding an uncomfortable power. Either way, this young man would leave with pain—either of social rejection or physical wound.

Pausing a moment to reflect on my dilemma, I mentally paddled back to the fork in the river that had towed me into this deep water. The last Public Health dentist had made his rounds two years ago at Tanana and along the Yukon. Since that time, all those in need of dental care either had to fly to Fairbanks or remain in pain. Both arrangements were less than ideal.

I should not have been surprised when Mary Ann, my spunky, new director of nurses, urged me to consider this crucial field of village medicine, and then one day presented me with my first dental patient. "Doctor, there is an elderly Native man in the waiting room. He has several large cavities and is in excrutiating pain. Can't you help him?"

"Well, Mary Ann, I really would like to help, but I do not have any dental experience, much less dental equipment," I said. Reluctantly, she relayed the message to the old man and sent him home with pain medication.

I thought my logic would silence her plea. Instead, it triggered a search, and like a group of kids on a treasure hunt, she and the others on the hospital staff spread out, searching the attic, basement, and old supply closets.

"Oh, Dr. Gaede, we found a whole drawer of dental instruments and something like a dental chair!" Mary Ann returned to my office with delight. "And by the way, here are several books on dentistry."

I'd wanted to be a bush pilot and a bush doctor-not a bush dentist. Nevertheless, my adventuresome spirit coupled with the patient's need pushed me through the classroom doors to "Bush Dentist 101."

Fortunately, the medical terminology, anatomical descriptions, and techniques were easy to understand. My three years of giving major anesthetics made the dental blocks relatively simple. I presented myself with honors when I ended my studies.

A few days later, I made the announcement: "All right, Mary

Tooth-pullin' time 105

Ann, I'm ready. Prepare my first victim—I mean patient."

Putting on an air of confidence and experience, I walked up the stairs to the second floor of the hospital and into the recently designated "dentist office." It was a small office without windows and contained a small number of white cupboards. Sam, the native man in distress, sat straight up in the black, cracked vinyl dentist chair. He had been living on aspirin and hope that I would treat him. Immediately he opened his mouth, pointing deep inside and groaning. My overhead light sought out the offending molar. Yes, I could understand his discomfort. So far, so good. I asked Sam to close his mouth for a moment.

"Sam, I'm going to give you something so you won't feel me pulling your tooth."

Without a sound, he endured the pokes of the needle. As we both waited for the dental block to take effect, I asked him about his family and his trap lines. Apparently the winter had favored him with full traps.

Then, gripping the forceps, I slowly loosened his tooth. A strong yank sent the bloody culprit flying out across the room. Mary Ann, Sam, and I smiled at one another in triumph.

"You'll feel a lot better now. Are any of the others giving you trouble?" I asked, trying to be casual. He shook his head in a vigorous "no." My career as bush dentist was successfully launched.

As fate would have it, my fame spread up and down the Yukon River. One morning as I was making hospital rounds, I heard dogs barking frantically at the front door. Before I could reach the door, a snow-covered Indian stumbled inside, leaving his dog team yapping on the hospital porch. A thick wolverine ruff obscured his face.

"Help . . . doctor . . . tooth," was all I could make out as he mumbled through frozen lips.

Five minutes later, the thawed-out middle-aged Indian man explained that a severe toothache had caused him to mush from Rampart, 80 miles upriver, to find a doctor. I removed the offending molar and then by his request, extracted two more teeth—as a preventive measure.

"Don't want to come back. Too cold and long," he told me. Pulling his ruff around his now-smiling face, he shook my hand, thanked me profusely, and disappeared out the door.

"Doctor?" the boy's insistent question drew me back to the

present. The sea of faces watched expectantly, and I felt the pressure of going ahead and making a decision.

Wishing for the wisdom of Solomon, I reluctantly agreed to torture the boy at his request. Immediately the villagers edged close around us, some with words of empathy, others shaking their heads in doubt. The drama before them was most likely the best entertainment available in the village.

Carefully, the village schoolteacher focused her flashlight as I took hold of and slightly loosened the tooth. The room was silent. The boy winced.

"Remember, I don't have any medicine to keep this from hurting," I told him. "You can still change your mind."

He shook his head, his eyes wide with anticipation. I loosened the tooth some more. Then, with a steady tug, the tooth departed from its socket.

The spectators cheered! The boy held his jaw. The other teenage boys rushed around him. He blinked his eyes hard, and then a smile slowly edged out of his mouth: acceptance rights were his.

I took the special tooth and gently added it to my pint jar. I was nearly as proud of these trophies as I was of my moose antlers and bearskins.

"Thanks doctor," the boy tugged at my sleeve.

"No problem, son," I said smiling at him and wiping the perspiration from my forehead. "No problem at all . . ."

15
Double-feature drama
March 1959

For three days ice fog had coated our world. The delicate white frost crystals hovered on the thermometer which read a harsh $-20°$ to $-40°$ F. "The ice fog has created severe electrical radio disturbances. I wonder what's happening in the down-river villages." My apprehension leaked out to my family at the supper table.

Much of my communication with the villages was with missionaries or schoolteachers via two-way radios. "Hey Doc, what do we do now?" would often blare over the two-way. Subsequently, I attempted to ask the "right" questions, make diagnoses, and suggest "over-the-phone" treatment. These rugged individuals loved the Native people and were sought out in times of medical emergencies, deaths, and various other crises. In addition to keeping me in touch with the 22 villages for which I was responsible, the radio calls connected the teachers and missionaries with a small piece of "civilization," which showed how isolated the villages were in comparison with Tanana.

Life in all of Alaska was tough—especially in winter when everything was locked in darkness, with only an occasional exit of a few feeble hours of midday grayness. Missionaries, especially women, encountered additional stresses. Since schools were not available in all the villages, missionaries had the challenge of home-schooling their children. With children crowding them all day in their small cabins, no favorite corner cafe to escape for a cup of tea and stimulating adult conversation, no variety of cooking ingredients, no library for new books, inevitably there was a natural progression toward "cabin fever."

We tried to encourage the missionaries. Often, our basement turned into a revolving-door "Tanana Holiday Inn," as pregnant missionary women would come with their children to await the arrival of another child—or families would just "get out" of their villages. We became well acquainted as we all shared one bathroom and our children found trouble together. One too-quiet afternoon, Ruby caught Mark and a three-year-old missionary child in the act of throwing thick-yolked eggs down the basement hallway.

We would also take "missionary journeys" down the Yukon, carrying along news, sharing books, and offering social support.

On this occasion, communication with the villages finally broke through the silence with a telephone call from Tanana FAA: there was a medical crisis at Kaltag, where I'd recently practiced my dentistry skill. Kaltag had desperately tried to reach the Tanana hospital by two-way radio, but when that was not possible, they tried an alternate means of communication through the Galena FAA, which was often capable of relaying information during weather difficulties. No luck. Still undaunted, Kaltag tried the Bethel FAA, which then leapfrogged the message to Tanana FAA, and then to our hospital.

The message: A child is in a coma and needs immediate medical attention. Can Dr. Gaede fly in?

The reply: Weather permitting, Dr. Gaede will be there as soon as possible.

Mercy flights were not difficult in the summer land of the midnight sun, but in the winter? The frozen sun stiffly pulled itself up above the treetops at about 10 A.M., only to fall away sharply around 2 P.M., plunging the arctic world back into dark coldness. These winter flights could be treacherous.

For two days I paced around the hospital waiting for the fog to lift. "Mary Ann, are you ready for a mercy flight?" I asked, handing her a list of medical supplies to pack for our mission. Meanwhile, I checked and rechecked my ambulance-red Family Cruiser, making sure it would be ready to take off.

In winter, I babied my plane, which was equipped with skis and tied down on the Yukon River in front of our house. The engine was constantly swaddled with heavy blankets to hold in the heat provided by an electric heater; the oil was carried indoors, ready to be warmed and fed back to the engine at a moment's notice. After freeze-up, the river had provided a solid airstrip, but the pressure ridges jutting up turned the prospect into a mission impossible. "Pete, can you fire up the CAT?" I asked. He accepted the challenge and the 12-ton D8 CAT lumbered out onto the four-foot ice, smoothing out what had been in my children's eyes an arctic expedition playground.

At 9:30 on the third morning, four days after the Kaltag child had gone into a coma, the ice fog subsided, although the temperature remained at −30° F. Dressed in heavy army parkas with thick red fox ruffs around our faces, white "bunny boots," and other survival gear, Mary Ann and I climbed into the plane for our flight for life.

After two hours of trailing the Yukon River, we landed on the river in front of Kaltag. A group of Indians crowded around us as we unloaded the medical supplies and drained the engine oil into a two-gallon can to be taken inside and heated before the return flight.

Quietly the soft-soled mukluked villagers padded on the snow as they escorted us to a log cabin. Hopeless death chant wails enveloped us as we entered the cabin, where nearly a dozen people accompanied the sick child's parents—all resigned to the death of the child.

Upon examination of the 13-year-old boy, I realized the prognosis was indeed grim. Not only was the boy in a coma, but he was dehydrated with a temperature of 105° F, a very rapid pulse, and one lung nearly filled with fluid. Convulsing intermittently, he made an occasional feeble effort to cough.

His parents filled me with other information: he was an epileptic, and because of a recent cold, resulting in bronchitis and loss of appetite, he had stopped eating and discontinued his dilantin and phenobarbital. As a result, his convulsions had increased and he had became comotose. Besides all this, I suspected that he might have active tuberculosis, since Kaltag had been hard-hit by this disease.

Once the diagnosis had been formed, Mary Ann and I began emergency treatment, surrounded by a group of quiet, but now curious onlookers. Dehydration was the number one problem, so we administered an intravenous eletrolyte and glucose solution followed by a glucose and water solution. A gastric tube was inserted for giving dilantin, phenobarbital, and massive doses of penicillin. Intramuscular injections of penicillin came next.

As we concentrated on the critical need in this cabin, a second medical crisis was developing in another part of the village. Rose Nabinger, the missionary wife, now six months pregnant, had been spotting for several days. (Her husband, Don, and seven-year-old daughter, were at Unalakleet speaking at the Covenant High School.) Later she told me she'd prayed, "Dear God, please send me medical help!"

As I was finishing up caring for the boy and waiting for the medication to take effect, I shrugged the tension from my neck and shoulders. "For some reason I feel I should go see the Nabingers," I said to Mary Ann. There wasn't much more I could do for the boy, and the village was small enough in case Mary Ann needed to reach me.

I knocked on the Nabinger's cabin door. No one seemed to be there. I knocked again and then the door creaked open. "Thank God! You came!" Rose startled me with her sudden exclamation. After she explained her problem, I examined her. A miscarriage was imminent. "Just relax—I'll be right back," I calmly instructed her, then uncalmly rushed out the door to race back across the snowy trail to the first patient.

Except for the boy's parents, the house was now empty. Mary Ann greeted me with a smile, "He's stable now," Gathering up my medical supplies, I whispered gruffly, "Grab your parka and follow me—we've got another house call to make."

Back at the Nabingers, Mary Ann added more wood to the 50-gallon barrel stove and heated water. After several hours, Rose expelled the small, dead fetus. The crisis, however, was not over. Bleeding profusely, Rose's blood pressure dropped while her pulse rate increased. My precious medical supplies were quickly depleted, and improvisation was imperative. I filled an empty IV bottle with boiling water, added a teaspoon of salt, cooled this solution in the snow, and administered it to my patient.

The night eventually stretched into morning as Mary Ann returned to the boy and I remained with Rose. Gradually both patients showed signs of improvement and stability.

By forenoon, the hazy sun fought off the tenacious ice fog, making our return flight to Tanana possible. After a last-minute "hospital round" at the Nabinger's, we poured the warmed engine oil back into the crankcase, scraped the frost off the wings, and removed a seat from the plane. We managed to fit the groggy boy inside two mummy sleeping bags and into the plane.

The plane crunched down the hard-packed snow of the river airstrip and lifted into the air. At 2,000 feet I contacted the Galena FAA, relaying our flight plan and expected arrival time to Tanana FAA.

The antiquated, yet faithful ambulance, our primary source of on-land transportation, met the plane on the river landing strip, transferring the young patient to the hospital.

My suspicions were confirmed—the boy had active tuberculosis pneumonia. Within a few weeks he recovered sufficiently from his pneumonia and epilepsy to be transferred to the Anchorage Native Hospital for extended treatment.

"Well, Dr. Gaede, that was a close one, and twice as much as we'd expected," Mary Ann pondered out loud. "I wasn't sure we'd make it there in time—and then that missionary lady, wasn't that uncanny how just when she needed you, you happened to be in the village?"

I knew deep inside that this hadn't "just happened," but that I'd witnessed a miracle of God's love and power in this double feature. There was a greater Physician than myself to help in these kinds of dramas.

16
The last Alaskan nomads
April 1959

Crouching down, I moved through the darkness, feeling my way along in the low tunnel-like entry to the house. Gingerly, I withdrew my hand from a husky's furry body. Walking in this position was nearly impossible. Three days, before, I'd developed a sciatic nerve irritation and now every step sent excrutiating pain up my left leg. Medication deadened this pain, but I was more than ready to stand up straight. Finally, my Eskimo host tugged at a door. A kerosene lantern illuminated a typical 20-by-18 foot one-room dwelling, with twigs covering the floor and caribou hides piled up in one corner.

I'd just finished a day of medical examinations in the Eskimo village of Anaktuvuk Pass, and my assistant, Anna Bortel—a schoolteacher from Tanana—and I were now guests of one of the villagers. Even with all my previous travels to Alaskan villages, this was a new experience.

The Anaktuvuk Pass Eskimos were literally "people of the caribou." The majority of the Eskimos lived along the upper coast of Alaska. The Anaktuvuk Pass Eskimos were an exception. Until recently, they moved in tandem with the migrating caribou through the Brooks Range, eating caribou, wearing caribou, and living in temporary caribou tents. Anaktuvuk Pass was only a passageway and campsite until 1951, when a post office was established. Just last year, in 1958, a community Presbyterian church was constructed. Having an official address and a structure to worship in apparently influenced the Eskimos to modify their nomadic lifestyle.

An as yet unchanged unique feature of this village was its total isolation; unlike most Alaskan villages, it had no river highway to connect it with other villages, nor did it lie along the coast, with access to other villages by boat. Futhermore, there was no airstrip. Only small planes with floats to land on the lake in the summer and skis in the winter provided a tenuous lifeline to the outside world. These Eskimos depended on dogsleds for transportation in the winter. The restrictions limited food provisions and other necessary supplies to the village. Truly, Anaktuvuk was one of Alaska's most secluded villages.

"Sit there," said Arthur, motioning toward the caribou skins.

As I moved past the stove toward the skins, I noticed a pan with dark water. Arthur dipped water from a five-gallon water can and added it to the pan on the stove. He threw a handful of loose tea into the black liquid and turned on the flame.

In spite of the dirt floor, the room was warm, and we pulled off our heavy wool gloves and unzipped our parkas. I tried to find a comfortable position for my leg on the pile of skins. "Doc, isn't this a wonderful experience?" whispered Anna, as Arthur opened a box of flat, round pilot boy crackers. Our eyes roamed around the room, spotting a caribou skin mask fastened to the thick sod wall. A miniature kayak, tipped on its side on the table, lay beside an ulu knife and a rounded pile of sinew string.

During my 1½ years at Tanana, I'd visited all the 22 villages of my assigned area except Anaktuvuk Pass. This village, in the heart of the Brooks Range, and a two-hour flight north of Tanana, did not have a schoolteacher or a resident missionary, so communication was limited. Besides the fact that it had been several years since a physician had visited the village, I was curious about these seminomadic, inland Eskimos. I decided that an April trip up north would benefit them and me.

"Yes, and aren't you glad you came along?" I chuckled in response to Anna's question. "Now you'll have more great stories to re-create for your students."

Anna was a family friend and Naomi and Ruth's schoolteacher. Instead of reading stories to the students, Anna would often make up her own, blending real Alaskan tales and fantastic make-believe. The stories would be continued from day to day and were as fascinating and suspenseful as any TV show the children could wish for. But story-telling was not the reason Anna had come along.

Anna always seemed to have her ear to the ground about teaching news and her eye out for adventure. She had heard about the Anaktuvuk Eskimos from a visiting public health nurse who suggested that Anna accompany our medical team on our next visit. Immediately, Anna had requested unpaid leave to go with the team. The State Department of Education wired back a message to go and take a census of school-aged children in this remote village where no school existed. Exuberantly, Anna joined us.

Arthur graciously held out blue melmac mugs of steaming tea, and we cautiously sipped the strong brew as it fogged up our glasses. "Arthur, how often do people fly into Anaktuvuk Pass?" I asked, thinking of his kind hospitality.

"The mail plane comes once a week," he replied. "And the Presbyterian missionary comes every two weeks or so—he flew in this afternoon, you know." He was quiet for a moment and then continued. "Many people are afraid to fly in the Brooks Range mountains. Right now a white man is lost up there."

"And last fall a Fish and Wildlife team disappeared," I added.

While Anna talked with Arthur about the village children, I thought of our flight over. After we had fueled at Bettles, we'd followed the John River through the Brooks Range. The expansive valley rose to tall, steep gray granite cliffs, and everywhere the snow was windswept clean and smooth. Trees that had clumped together joined as couples, then stood individually, until even those short brave survivors diminished into sporadic dwarfed bushes. The stark white beauty against the blue sky belied the danger of the country. This was no place to get lost or be forced down. The FAA personnel warned us that Anaktuvuk Pass was easy to miss. "You can fly right over it—even if you use the John River for a landmark and guide."

As we had flown through the valley, which was swept clean except for solitary patches of stunted wllows tossed here and there across the two- to four-mile expanse, I had wondered, "How can any living thing survive in this arctic plain?"

When we'd neared the area where I expected to find Anaktuvuk Pass, I had dropped the plane down over the river. Sure enough, there was a village of about 20 buildings, clumped together against the raw elements. Oddly enough, one log building was a part of the tiny community. Since Anaktuvuk Pass was 40 miles above timberline, all wood was at a premium and had to be hauled in by dogsled. I was curious about the number of trips it must have taken to haul in all the logs for this building—and the motivation for doing so.

We circled and took pictures, and I scouted around trying to find a suitable landing strip. I finally settled for the large frozen lake about a half-mile east of the village. "The snow looks drifted and crusty," I said over the engine's roar. "Hang on."

After the initial impact of touchdown, the plane slid up and down along the hard drifts until I cut the engine. Parka-clad adults and children with bright red cheeks swarmed around us in the stiff wind.

"There are maybe 20 or 30 children who would go to school," said Arthur to Anna. "Before now they go to boarding school at Wrangell. They get hold of liquor at school. We don't want that. Anaktuvuk Pass is a dry village."

I had seen many of those children during the afternoon as I began examining the 96 villagers. Between the lake and the village was a large military shelter well, where I conducted my clinic, and where we slept and ate. We hung up blankets to ensure some privacy for the physical examinations, but it seemed we were more concerned about modesty than were our patients.

Just that morning, two Public Health nurses had arrived and had spent the morning giving tuberculosis skin tests and polio shots. The main problems were chronic ear infections and recurrent respiratory infections. I was surprised at the small amount of tuberculosis as contrasted with the Indian villages.

"I think it is time now for church," said Arthur, standing up and reaching for his parka. The fur of the parka was turned inwards, and colorful cloth parkas were worn over these drab caribou parkas.

Before standing up to leave, I started to drain my cup of tea. Looking into the bottom of my cup, I changed my mind: this thickened mixture must have been steeping for days.

We left the warmth of the house, and stepped out into the cold. Just last week, $-40°$ F temperatures had repaid a visit to this frigid wilderness where springtime hesitated to show her face.

The wind whipped our fur ruffs across our faces as we climbed up the knoll above the village toward the log building—a partially finished church. For some reason, I expected to find pews inside, but as usual, there were willow boughs on the floor. People poured inside and matter of factly sat on the floor. They enthusiastically sang in English out of a familiar-looking brown hymm book, and then proceeded into a full-scale church service, complete with baptism, communion, and church membership.

The service concluded at 10:30 P.M. and as we walked out into the below-zero wind and down the hill to the shelter well, the bright moon was just peaking over the tall mountains in the distance, casting a silver sheen over the village. All was silent except for the wind. I wondered if these people ever got used to the wild beauty, and if this beauty was compensation for the rigors of the environment.

Our medical crew turned our examining rooms into sleeping quarters. I awkwardly manuveured into my narrow army surplus mummy bag with my bunny boots still on. Because of my pain, I was unable to bend down and remove my bunny boots or heavy wool pants. I chided myself about my difficulties. I was more used to being the doctor than the patient.

After completing medical examinations the next day, we prepared to leave. The people seemed to think nothing of the continual marrow-chilling wind and hovered around us, escorting us to the plane. Sometimes they would walk backwards to keep the wind off their faces, and always they smiled. The children walked on top of the snow, which was hard-packed from the wind.

We said farewells with handshakes, pats on the backs, and more smiles. Very carefully, I pulled myself into the plane and adjusted the weight on my left leg. The blowing parkas of our send-off crew served as multicolored windsocks, and I turned the plane toward the ever-blowing wind.

Anna pressed her face against the window and waved until the people were dark dots against the white background. Then she sat in silence. I wasn't sure if she was thinking of future possibilities at Anaktuvuk Pass or just gathering in the white polished wonderment of the Brooks Range valley and mountains.

After a brief fueling stop at Bettles, we hurried back to Tanana. Although Tanana was reported as clear, gray clouds were settling into the Ray Mountains. I avoided the mountains and instead took a valley to the west. Like a magnet, the clouds followed us as we traced a river's path beneath the low ceiling and snuck into Tanana.

"Tanana is so plush!" exclaimed Anna, when we climbed out of the plane. "A grocery store, school, hospital, running water and electricity, an airstrip, trucks . . ."

Such talk continued as we walked the short distance from the river landing strip.

All four children were at the living room window watching for us. Knowing how I usually brought back souvenirs from many of my trips, they clamored, "What did you bring us?"

I pulled out red fox and wolverine furs, and then a caribou mask. They giggled as they took turns trying on the mask.

"And wait until you see our pictures," I said. "You won't believe how the Eskimo women carry their babies. They carry them inside their parkas on their backs."

"Don't they just fall out?" asked Naomi.

"They put a belt around their parkas, which catches the babies under their bottoms. It makes a little seat to ride on," I explained.

"Yes, and guess how they get the babies out?" laughed Anna. "They don't just undo the belt and let the babies drop out. No, the mothers lean over with their heads nearly to their knees and the babies come out the top of the parkas where their mothers gently catch them." Anna tried to demonstrate and everyone laughed.

"And that's not all," I said. "The babies don't have anything on their bottoms."

"No diapers?!" said Ruby, Naomi and Ruth in unison.

"Yes. I didn't know that and asked a mother to demonstrate for me so I could take a picture," exclaimed Anna. "So she, did. Right outside in the wind and cold."

"No!" repeated our captive audience.

"Yes! I was shocked," said Anna. "The mothers' parkas are caribou skin lined and they wipe the caribou hairs off their babies' faces, while the babies blink their little dark eyes in the cold brightness. Of course I asked her to put the baby away. She pulled her parka up, pushed him around to her back, bent over until he slid up her back, and then belted him in."

We agreed to get together as soon as our pictures were developed and invite over other friends to see our excursion to the last nomads of the north. Before Anna returned to her school apartment, Ruby offered her a cup of tea. "Not right now, thanks," said Anna, glancing at me with an amused look.

"It's hard to believe that such a different world is only two hours away," I said to no one in particular. I looked around me. A plush green carpet, rather than twigs and branches, covered the floor. There were no caribou skins to sit on, but chairs accompanied the kitchen table. I walked into the living room and eased into a soft chair. "Naomi and Ruth, could you help me out and untie my bunny boots?" I asked. "I've had them on for three days now."

At the time, I didn't suspect that I would return to Anaktuvuk Pass and discover that a baby had been named for me—not only using my first name of "Elmer," but a middle name of "Gaede." Neither did I know that within a year Anna would return to Anaktuvuk Pass to establish a school and be the first schoolteacher, as well as help the Eskimos market their native crafts and make Anaktuvuk Pass known for their masks, and have even more stories to tell—enough to fill a book of her own.

I did know that, as much as I loved to make and gather Alaskan stories of flying adventures, medical excitement, and hunting tales, it was nice for a change to just enjoy Alaska's natural beauty and the uniqueness of her people.

17
℞ for excitement: Mix flying with medicine
May 1959

"Doc, we have a big problem. Do you think you could fly down?" On this particular afternoon, I was talking over the two-way radio with Russ Arnold, Arctic Missions missionary at the village of Ruby. I never knew what I'd hear when I opened on the air with "This is KIK 731, Tanana; standing by for medical traffic."

Russ clued me in fast. "This woman, Roberta, has really gone beserk," he said. "She's smashing her furniture, screaming, and threatening to kill anyone who comes near her. Some of us have tried to calm her down, but nothing's working. We don't know what to do and we're afraid she'll harm herself—or someone else. Could you help us?"

Glancing out the window, I replied, "O.k. Russ, the weather looks good. I'll try to be there in an hour and a half." With the warmth and 24-hour daylight, summer "house calls," unlike winter house calls, were usually as simple as making hospital rounds.

As I walked down the hospital corridor to find Mary Ann, I tried to imagine what was in store for us. One thing was certain: mixing flying with medicine increased the chances for excitement. As I've already related, I'd added the emergency landing on my way to help Charlie at Manley Hot Springs, and if I hadn't flown into Kaltag and instead waited for the comotose boy to be airlifted to Tanana, I wouldn't have gotten in on the duo drama with Rose. On the negative side, sometimes when I was out making village "house calls," emergencies occurred at my homebase hospital.

Such was the case when I was at Galena and the nurses at Tanana sent word through FAA that a 2 1/2-year old boy was possibly dying here at my hospital. I jumped in the plane and chased up the Yukon as fast as I could. Darkness pursued me, then passed me by. When I got to Tanana, everything was black, and I couldn't find my clear, smooth river runway. To take a stab in the dark would be suicide since rugged pressure ridges surrounded the clear area. I flew around and around the village, trying to find a solution in my "hangar talk" mental file.

Then I saw it. First a flicker, then a growing bonfire on the river. I flew closer. Another flicker, a flame, and a fire at the other end of my runway. Someone had heard the continuous drone of the plane and figured out my plight. I found out later that Ruby had just left the Gronning's house when she noticed a plane circling overhead. "How will it ever see to land?" she asked our children as they walked together. About that time, she overheard two Native boys say , "That's the doctor's plane."

"No! He's in Galena," she said, trying to squelch the fear in her heart. It must have been a sight to see her race back to my riverbank parking spot, pulling a red sled with Mark and Mishal stuffed into a box, and Naomi and Ruth running alongside holding the box in place—five mufflers catching hot breath and flying back behind five red fox ruffed parka hoods.

By the time they reached the plane and touched the still warm cowling, I was already in the hospital. As was the pattern with many Natives, the parents had kept the child at home until death was imminent and then had brought him to the hospital to die. Unfortunately, my efforts had proved futile.

I hoped our efforts today would be successful, and when I located Mary Ann, I described the situation at the village of Ruby. "I want you to come with me, since you, as a woman, will be more able than me to calm down this patient and persuade her to take medication."

"I imagine you'd like *me* to escort her back on the charter plane, too," said Mary Ann, reading my thoughts.

Mary Ann packed medical supplies and I called to see if a charter would be available to fly the woman back to Tanana. We loaded my red pride and joy and within minutes, my tundra tires stirred up a dusty trail, then rotated to a stop in the air.

I'd flown up and down the Yukon so many times that while my eyes followed the flowing river, my mind naturally flowed off into other channels. As I glanced down at a kicker boat, my eyes moved past the chubby tundra tire. Once a pilot was up in the air, it was always reassuring to have the security that he could come back down. More specifically, I liked seeing my tire where it should be; in contrast to my first winter here when I looked down and saw my ski hanging with the front edge tilted down, ready to trip me when I landed.

"Hey, Doc!" I remembered hearing ex-chief Alfred Grant. "Your left ski looks funny."

"Looks like a broken cable." I assessed the problem.

We were six miles south of Tanana, after a previous aborted flight due to problems with an obstruction of the airspeed indicator. We seemed destined not to complete this simple trip south to Alfred's beaver trapline and some caribou feeding grounds. Once again, we turned around and fought our way back to Tanana through strong winds. Unlike the Family Cruiser, the J-3 did not have a radio so I couldn't describe my plight or needs to FAA. I circled around and around Tanana, hoping they could hear me above the rude, interferring wind— and also recognize my problem.

After being tossed around like a kite for some time, several men carrying fire extinguishers hurried out of the FAA station and toward the middle of the runway. My plan was to land on my right ski, which could cost me my right wing, but not our lives. It looked as if the men planned to put out a resulting fire. Unknown to all of us, there was another plan. Anna Bortel heard the wind, saw my dangling ski, and while I repeatedly circled Tanana, she frantically ran circles in her school apartment not knowing what to do—except pray. Her plan was that God would still the wind and protect me from an accident.

Anna's plan worked—or God's plan. Just before touching down, I jerked the stick back to try to swing the left ski tip forward before stalling on my right ski. It worked. I touched down on both skies. The ski moved into its proper position, remaining secure as I brought the plane to a careful stop beside the FAA men.

"Boy, were you lucky, Doc," they said in near unison.

I didn't exactly agree about the luck I recognized a miracle when I saw one.

Mary Ann brought me back to the present, patting me on the arm and pointing below to a bear catching fish at the mouth of a small incoming river.

Within an hour, we'd covered the 125 miles to Ruby, circled the small village of 60 to 110 people, and landed on the village strip, which was a rolling hill with a crest in the center. Russ met us with a, "So glad you're here, Doc." He hastily escorted us through a group of curious villagers to Roberta's nearby cabin. From the outside, it was a typical cabin with a gas-powered washing machine setting on the front porch.

I was surprised by the silence as we stood cautiously in the open doorway. Russ remained outside while Mary Ann and I moved slowly inside. My eyes gradually adjusted to the darkness and focused on a older woman slouched on a shelflike sleeping bench against the far wall of the one-room cabin. Without acknowledging our presence, she sat sullen and disheveled. I introduced myself and Mary Ann, then quietly tried to talk to her about her frustrations and anger, as I inched toward her. A red vinyl covered kitchen chair served as a barrier between us, so I pulled it to one side and sat down. Mary Ann stood behind me.

"Wouldn't you like to just get away from your home and family for a few days and rest in the hospital?" I gently asked.

She made no verbal response, but pulled back, tucking her legs beneath her and pressing her body against the wall.

"We're here to help you." said Mary Ann.

No response.

I shifted my attention from Roberta to the broken white dishes on the wide-planked floor, dirty clothes strewn around the room, and a wooden chair smashed against the cold barrel stove. Concerned that she would erupt into the behavior previously described by Russ, I wanted to give her tranquilizers.

I tried again. "Roberta, I'd like you to . . ."

"No!" she screamed. Swinging her feet off the bench, she stared at me wildly, poised for flight out of the cabin.

Now what? I could understand Russ's helpless feeling. I leaned my body toward her path of escape, and resumed talking in soft and hopefully soothing tones. After what seemed as long as an Alaskan summer day, she consented to go to the Tanana hospital. With relief, I stood up and announced, "Roberta, I've arranged for a plane to take you to the Tanana hospital. You just need to pack a suitcase and we'll go down to the river where the charter will come in on floats." I'd sighed too quickly.

Roberta scowled at us and loudly blurted out, "I won't go anywhere unless it's with you, Doctor Gaede!"

"No, Roberta, that will not be possible." I felt as if I were dealing with a child. "I will meet you in Tanana when you fly in on the charter."

"No! No! No!" she shrieked, stamping her feet and shaking her head until her undone braids struck her in the face.

I was afraid she'd start throwing things or run out of the room, but instead, she dissolved into a sobbing heap on the filthy floor. "I'll be good. I'll be good. Don't leave me."

I motioned to Mary Ann to follow me and walked outside into the bright sunshine. Taking a deep breath of the fresh air, I bombarded her with questions. "Do you have any ideas? What would happen if we couldn't get her on a charter? What would happen if she were to fly back with us? What would this disturbed woman do in the confines of a small plane?" After weighing the alternatives, I decided to go ahead with an emergency flight. We did, however, need to map out our strategy for any in-flight crises.

"Roberta will sit in front with me, and you will sit behind her with a filled syringe of a hypnotic drug. That will calm her."

When we reentered the cabin, Roberta stood waiting beside her suitcase. Russ and several Indian men trailed behind us as Mary Ann and I kept Roberta between us in our march toward the plane. We all found our designated seats. Roberta docilely buckled up and with a sign of resignation folded her hands in her lap. No problems so far.

The plane rapidly climbed into the calm blue, cloud-smudged sky. About five miles out of Ruby we were at 2,000 feet above the Yukon. Without warning, our compliant passenger exploded! Grabbing the plane door handle, she frantically shoved open the door and with a desperate lunge thrust her foot out into the freezing air. "I'm going home!" she screamed. Now we had big problems.

Instinctively, I rolled the plane over to a steep left bank to keep my unwilling passenger from falling out. Mary Ann locked her arms around Roberta's neck as Roberta clawed at the door in an attempt to regain her balance and continue her escape. Meanwhile, the compass rotated wildly, the airspeed indicator crept down, and the turn-and-bank indicator slammed to an almost vertical position. It was like a rollercoaster ride in the air.

Then, with the 60-degree angle of the plane, the weight of the door created enough discomfort that Roberta retrieved her foot. The plane door slapped open and shut as the plane circled erratically in the untroubled sky. When Roberta again attempted to make an emergency exit "home," I shifted my position and with my left hand on the stick, I firmly hooked my right arm around her neck. "Give her the shot!" I yelled at Mary Ann, who was also trying to maintain her balance.

Manuevering in the cramped and pitching cabin made finding Roberta's thrashing arm an extraordinary challenge. After a seemingly endless struggle, the needle found its mark. Eventually, our patient relaxed and the plane door was again securely locked. Neither Mary Ann nor I felt relaxed or secure. For the last 100 miles, we flew in silence, not wanting to agitate our passenger.

Being a bush doctor, I never knew what to expect—on village house calls, in the hospital, or even in my own house. Last winter I was awakened in the middle of the night by "Doctor, doctor, Lucy's awfully sick." I couldn't believe my ears. It sounded as though the voice was nearly in my bedroom. Was I dreaming? I got out of bed, walked down the hall, and nearly bumped into an old white man in my kitchen. He waited for me to get dressed. I followed him down the snow-packed road to his house, where I examined Lucy, his native wife, who had pleurisy.

I'd never had someone make a doctor's appointment quite like that. Neither had I recieved the kind of payment which came my way a few days later. Ruby was at the hosptial and the old gent stopped her. "Are you the doctor's wife?" She nodded. "How is your potato supply?" Ruby told him that the only ones she had were frozen. That same day, he showed up on our doorstep with a peck of potatoes he'd grown the summer before. We both greatly appreciated his gratitude, but after that, Ruby did a double-check on the door locks before we went to bed.

Thinking of door locks, I looked over to see the plane door still locked. Tanana FAA had notified the hospital of our estimated time of arrival and the dilapidated ambulance waited in anticipation as we touched down. Roberta was initially treated at our hospital, then transferred to the Alaska Psychiatric Hospital in Anchorage.

"Well, Dr. Gaede, mixing your medical duties with flying certainly brought on some excitement today," mused Mary Ann as we settled Roberta into bed.

"Yes, the kind I like best when there is a safe ending. Now what was on today's schedule?" I asked jokingly.

I heard rapid footsteps coming down the hallway. "Dr. Gaede," the emergency room nurse said trying to catch her breath. "Mrs. Gronning was just admitted. She's miscarrying and hemorrhaging."

This was still not the time to relax.

18
The top of Alaska
July 1959

I felt restless. My log of Alaskan adventures had room for more experiences. Yes, I'd covered a lot of country, especially with the polar bear hunt, but there was still unexplored territory north of the Brooks Range. I wanted to touch and see and experience the top of Alaska.

Let me explain a part of this insatiable drive. After four years in the land I'd learned to love, I was transferring "Outside," to the lower '48. Now as I stood on the banks of the Yukon, watching a plane circle overhead, the call of the wild rang loudly in my ears.

I walked up dusty Front Street toward the house-chapel, exchanging "hellos" for "Hi, Docs."

"Mel, how would you like to go to Barrow with me?" I asked my missionary friend, who had shared other flying and hunting trips with me. I needed someone I could depend on, just in case I was forced down—not that I expected such trouble.

"Sounds great, Doc," he eagerly said. "What exactly do you have in mind?"

We planned our trek to the northernmost point of Alaska—and the United States—for July 8, and mapped out the 1,300-mile trip over Anaktuvuk Pass and through the Brooks Range to Barrow, and then back along the coastline. This time I didn't want to encounter a fuel shortage, so I packed in 20 gallons of extra aviation gas. We added over 100 pounds of emergency gear, including clothes, food, guns, and plane-repair equipment. In contrast to the stingy J-3, this four-place plane generously opened its doors to our needs. Furthermore, I'd replaced the 108 hp engine with a 125 hp one.

The week prior to our departure, Alaska showed her worst side, with high winds, electrical storms, and frequent rain squalls. The Yukon River beat in protest against the shore, and trees fell over in the woods and on the riverbanks. The unstable ceiling vacillated between 1,000 and 2,000 feet—too unpredictable for healthy flying conditions. Snow showers taunted the upper coast of Alaska. On the evening before the 8th, the daily FAA weather sequences offered us little hope of improvement.

I liked my life to be orderly, just like my appointment book, so I went to bed planning to carry through with my scheduled departure.

My optimism was rewarded. By 10:00 A.M., the low morning scud broke up and the ceiling lifted to 2,500 feet. The barometer crept up to nearly 30.00, and the Kotzebue coastal area showed clearing with westerly winds. The improvements spread and by 11:00 A.M., Anaktuvuk Pass was reported open.

I ran down to Mel's house. "Let's try it. The weather is the best it's been in ten days." The plane left the ground at noon and we were off to see the top of Alaska.

We skimmed under a low ceiling as we slipped through a pass in the towering Ray Mountains and broke out onto the flat, many-laked north side. Light rain showers accosted us and persisted to dog us as we flew over Bettles and toward the Brooks Range. Stringy rain-threatening gray clouds hung like a curtain before us. I called Bettle's radio for a pilot report. No report available. Umiat and Barrow reported favorable conditions, so I told Bettles that we would push on through.

As we advanced toward the pass, we discovered a strong southerly wind funneling above the turquoise-green John River, which cleared an open airway for us to tunnel through. Despite the intermittent drizzle, which beaded up on our front windows and streaked back along the sides, the ceiling held at 1,000 feet. As we neared Anaktuvuk Pass, the skies gradually lifted, but with this encouragement came violent 60 to 70 mph pass winds. The plane trembled in the unstable air and eagerly moved to higher smooth air as the dark clouds retreated and blue sky took their place.

Having successfully negotiated the pass, we took a compass heading toward Umiat, flying over turquoise mottled lakes which looked like huge cut and polished rock halves. Narrow rust-streaked rivers zig-zagged around the flat, treeless tundra, cutting it into pieces of spongy patchwork. This country copied itself over and over, making checkpoints difficult to identify. We were reassured of our whereabouts when we saw the blue Colville River, with its huge mile-long sandbars.

Umiat, an abandoned military field, with two Wien's Airline radio men stationed to assist the airline's planes, lay dead ahead. We landed there to refuel, after flying for three hours and being prodded along by a healthy 40 mph tailwind.
mph tailwind.

We were on our last leg and now flying over a myriad of nameless semi-frozen lakes and braided serpentine rivers. The progression of water to ice created a three-dimensional look of varying shades from pale aqua to teal blue to blue-black and green-black in these old lakes which each year struggled to thaw. After flying an hour, we spotted a checkpoint, Teshekpuk Lake, to our north. We were on course.

Hundreds of caribou roamed beneath us, blending in with the monochromatic beige-brown tundra, and adding interest to flying over this boundless arctic territory, which at moments resembled terrain from a science-fiction space story. As we approached the upper coast of the Arctic Sea, the lakes became larger and more elongated.

In the distance, we noticed a white bank of fog or low clouds. "What do you think that is?" I asked Mel.

When we drew closer, we realized that this whiteness was actually the tremendous ice pack shoved up against the shore.

"Look! There's Barrow right ahead of us," he said excitedly.

We'd made it. The top of the world sprawled out about a mile along the shoreline. We circled over the beach and tried to find a place to land since there was only a military airport where pilots needed prior permission to land. We flew over the beach, but boats, dead walrus, or ice chunks obstructed our proposed runway. As we looked around for alternatives, I decided on the deeply rutted road in the fine soft beach sand at the Bowerville end of Barrow. Lowering the flaps, we settled down slowly with the tundra tires riding over the ruts.

A small group of laughing, chubby-cheeked Eskimo children surrounded the plane before Mel and I even stepped out into the clear, breezy air. So this was Barrow. I was eager to go exploring, but the winds shaking the plane reminded me that first we needed to tie down. Looking around, the only possibilities we found were a "honey" barrel and two small barrels of sand.

We started walking toward Barrow, the largest Eskimo settlement in North America, with a population of 800 to 1,000. After asking questions and directions, we were able to locate Miss Felkirchner who had been the Tanana School principal a year ago, and was now teaching here. Cordially she welcomed us and wanted to know all about Tanana, Anna Bortel, and some of her former students. She offered us beds to throw our sleeping bags on, provided a caribou roast supper, and proved to be a knowledgeable tour guide.

The "midnight sun" had risen on May 10 and would not set until August 2, so walking around after supper allowed unlimited daylight for sight-seeing. We soon discovered that "honey" barrels were a common sight in this impenetrable permafrost country, where sewer lines and any underground utilities, such as water, were impossible. To dispose of the sewage, everyone, including the villagers, Public Health Service hospital, and Bureau of Indian Affairs grade school, accumulated the waste in large barrels and then hauled them out onto the tundra. Water was a precious commodity and hauled in from the fresh-water lakes in the form of liquid or ice.

The cemetery revealed another problem. Some of the caskets sat above the ground with a few strips of tundra draped around them. In other spots, where the unpredictable permafrost had given way, the caskets had gradually and awkwardly fallen into the ground.

Permafrost formed when more cold entered the ground in the winter than could be pulled out in the summer. Permafrost actually created a solid foundation for houses; however, heat on the permafrost would "ruin" this sturdy foundation. Therefore, many of the houses sat on 4- to 5-foot pilings so that the house heat would not thaw the ground beneath them and they would not end up tilting unevenly on this semi-thawed foundation. Gardening was obviously impossible and drainage was another problem. Permanent gray puddles interrupted all the roads and paths. Farther from the shoreline, tundra flowers hid in short surprises of pink and yellow on the treeless terrain.

Much to our disappointment, we found that Barrow was highly geared for tourist attraction. Wiens Airline, which had an agreement with the military airstrip, had daily tourist flights connecting with Fairbanks, and one of Barrow's businessmen appeared to have a monopoly on the hotels and restaurants. Since Mel and I had flown in on a private plane and stayed outside the customary lodging places, we were given the cold shoulder. For instance, we couldn't get information about sightseeing, where to get gas, and so on.

Every evening during the summer, a group of Eskimos showed off their talents and traditions by demonstrating a blanket toss, performing Eskimo dances, and offering dogsled rides. The "blanket" was made of a large, round, ten- to fourteen-foot-diameter skin. It was a colorful display as approximately ten to fourteen adults and children in bright red, blue, and yellow parkas held on to the sides of the blanket with one person jumping in the middle of this trampoline.

For this evening, a young woman in a red parka showed off her skill and beauty. She warmed up with short jumps to see how high she could go. It was said that the blanket toss was originally used in spotting whales or other animals in the distance. The group of people around the blanket pulled back on the blanket sides after she come down, therefore helping to toss her back into the air. Her "team" and the crowd cheered her upward. This was not an individual "sport." Everyone worked together.

The dogsled rides were a definite tourist attraction, but after my real-life experiences, such as the ride into Lime Village, the glamour was gone for me. Even though it was not uncommon for Barrow to have snow showers in the summer, there was insufficient snow on the ground for the dogs to pull the sleds. Being resourceful, the Eskimos attached small wheels to the sled runners, and the smiling husky dogs pulled the smiling tourists around the village.

After awhile, we ended our wanderings around the village and our interesting conversations with Miss Feldkirshner, and went to bed, despite the daylight.

About 5:00 A.M., shrill high-pitched screeching wind woke me up. It sounded like a storm was working into a fury. A chill went down my back as I thought of my plane anchored near the water's edge, exposed to the full force of the wind—and water. I roughly shook Mel. "Get dressed. We've got to get to the plane!"

Blinding sand from the 50 mph gale scratched our faces and filled our eyes when we opened the door and made our way down the road toward the plane. The ice pack had moved out and the ice cakes thrashed around in the tumbling ocean.

"How are we going to get through, Doc?" Mel shouted. Before us, 40 to 50 feet of ice-choked water covered the road and blocked our path to the plane. I squinted my eyes against the sandy wind and followed the length of the water. My heart thudded loudly in my ears as I realized that the water had become a channel between the ocean and a lake just off shore—my plane now lay cut off from my rescue attempts. In my mind, I saw my pride and joy torn by ice and wind, and either submerged in salt water or littered across the beach.

"Mel, I can't give up," I said hoarsely. "I'm going to walk around."

"Doc, there's no way you can do that," said Mel, grabbing at my arm.

I pulled away, tucked my head down from the wind, and started along the water's edge. Nature tried to deter me as my boots sunk into the wet sand and the wind tore at my khaki pants and army parka. When I looked up for a moment to get my bearings, I saw ahead of me an elevated four-inch pipeline bridging the channel of water to dry land. Shakily, I straddled the pipe and slowly inched above the ice-filled turbulent water. Once on the other side, I attempted to run against the unrelenting wind.

To my relief, the plane was upright and untouched by the frothing water, even though one of my tie-downs had torn loose, allowing the tail to swing out toward the ocean. The broad wings bounced about, but the tires remained rooted securely in the sand. I quartered the plane back into the wind and searched for more tie-owns. Some large chunks of heavy scrap iron had been carried in with the storm, and they made excellent tie-downs.

About the time I secured my plane, several Eskimo men and women came out to check their skin boats, which were tied up along the water's edge. The high breakers loaded with enormous ice cakes had covered and damaged several boats. Together, we worked and salvaged their boats. They returned to the other end of the beach, which connected with Bowerville, and I made my way back the same way I'd come.

I felt as though I'd put in a day's work when I stumbled back into Miss Felkirchner's kitchen. "Looks as though you could use some hot breakfast" she said cheerily, flipping pancakes and pouring me a cup of steaming tea. After removing my wet, sandy boots, I fell into a kitchen chair and replenished my energy.

Getting socked in here was not my plan, so right after breakfast I checked into the forecasted weather. The courteous crew at the U.S. weather observation station offered us detailed information, although none was encouraging for our departure. The storm was forecast to remain at least a couple of days. We decided to make the most of our time, and since we hadn't completely toured the village the night before, we went back out into the gray air. Now that I knew my plane was secure, the wind didn't seem as fierce.

Either Eskimo children or adults followed us around so we were never without directions or guides—not that we could have gotten lost in this flat, one-road, sparsely built village. One old white man, at a general store, suspected we were new to the area and wouldn't let us leave until he'd told us about Barrow's history. "You know, boys, Barrow was named for Sir John Barrow of the British Admiralty by Captain Beechey of the Royal Navy in 1825." The old man sounded like a history book. "Yes, siree, that Captain Beechey was plotting the arctic coastline of North America. By the way, fellas, do you know the name of his ship?" He didn't pause to let us even guess. "HMS *Blossom*. Funny name for a ship up here, don't you think?" I think he could have spent the day talking to us, but finally after interrupting him with a "Thanks so much" and a friendly pat on the back, we continued our exploration.

Naturally I wanted to visit the Public Health Service hospital, and after that we invited ourselves over to Rev. John Chamber's, the Presbyterian "flying missionary of the North." Rev. Chamber's homebase was Barrow, but this pastor-pilot's parish was 40,000 square miles of tundra.

The next day, the winds abated to 25 to 30 mph, and the clouds held themselves up to 600 feet. A few local planes pushed against this ceiling, and we were told that we couldn't expect any better conditions. In addition to the weather difficulties, obtaining gas seemed to be an insurmountable challenge.

Local pilots all had their gas supply shipped in by boat. Since it was rare to have an outsider fly in, no store stocked gas. Finally, a local pilot working for the weather station suggested I try to get gas from Mr. Brower, the founder of adjacent Browerville, who owned most of the businesses in the area. Mr. Brower, an old man who was confined to his room, was reluctant to see us and a very discouraging person to talk to. I resorted to name-dropping, mentioning Miss Felkirchner, Rev. Chambers, and Public Health Service personnel.

Eventually he tired of begging and agreed to sell us one barrel of gas—if we could find a full barrel somewhere near his house. We searched, found a 55 gallon barrel, paid $1.25 per gallon, pumped the gas into our gas cans, and hauled it out to our plane. We'd overcome one obstacle, but now faced another.

When we took off, low scud prevented me from gaining much altitude, and I hovered at about 100 feet as I pointed the plane along the coastline. Eventually I would catch up to Point Hope and then retrace my route back from the polar bear hunt. To allow for the 30 mph crosswinds, I had to crab the plane, pointing its nose toward the wind, which gave the illusion of flying sideways.

Several miles south of Barrow we flew over the Will Rogers Monument, which commemorated the 1935 death of the American humorist and pioneer world-circuiting pilot. Rogers had landed there, seeking directions to Barrow. Upon takeoff, his plane rose 50 feet in the air, stalled, then plunged into the river below. Yesterday, I'd been offered $50 to fly a tourist to this monument. Even if I thought I'd get an adjacent monument, there was no way I would have attempted to take off in yesterday's storm.

After an hour and a half of following the sharp coastline, we came to Wainwright. I wanted to stop to visit the Wycliff Bible translators, so I checked out the narrow beach for landing. I eased the plane down, hampered by the stiff crosswind.

Everything seemed fine until after I landed and turned the plane toward the low shore banks. In spite of the large tundra tires, the plane bogged down into the unusual soft spot of mud and sand. From the air, I hadn't seen this draw from a slough, which was created by water runoff from the village. As had become typical, a group of Eskimo men hastened to our aid, and together we pulled the plane farther up the shoreline.

The stop was well worth our time. The tundra here at Wainwright was so soggy that the villagers had contructed "sidewalks" throughout the village. The sidewalks consisted of 50-gallon gas drums, turned on their sides and placed next to one another. On top of them, were planks to provide a flat surface for walking. I had never seen or heard of such ingenuity, and I added this to my 16 mm documentary. An hour's worth of conversation and a cup of tea refreshed us, and we pulled out of the miry landing strip and back into the air.

The weather conditions steadily improved. No crosswind. Clear sky. High altitude. Flying seemed too easy. Over Point Lay. Past Cape Beaufort. Then it happened.

"What's that white stuff?" I asked Mel, sensing danger, but not knowing exactly why. A solid wall of white crept toward us from the ocean, closing off forward visiblity. Was it fog or low clouds? We approached the edge of this eerie wall. Within seconds, I recognized the whiteness. "It's a blizzard!"

Immediately, I executed a 180-degree turn and, breaking out in a sweat searched wildly for an emergency landing spot. My mind snapped out a picture of a sod cabin along the beach, about 12 miles or so back. I opened the throttle to race the storm. We approached our possible refuge with the storm ready to engulf us. There was no time to drag the narrow shale beach, so I hurriedly set the plane down, taxiing up near the sod cabin, before cutting the throttle.

Within seconds, the blizzard struck and the gale whipped the breakers over our plane tracks. "Mel, we've got to get the plane to higher ground!" Tugging and pushing frantically, we managed to move the plane out of the ocean's grasp. We filled our emergency gunny sacks with rocks, tied down the plane, and made our way to the cabin.

Apparently getting caught in these storms was not uncommon, and the good samaritan cabin provided us with the basic needs of safety, cases of army rations, firewood and a Yukon stove, and clean planking on which to throw down our sleeping bags. Immediately, we started a fire in the easy to disassemble man-made rectangular iron stove, used both for heat and cooking.

By morning, the blizzard had worn itself out and visibility was up to one mile. Takeoff did present a problem, however. I had to follow a tight line with one wing over the water and the other over tundra. The high breakers shared with me less than 600 feet of the shore, forcing me to use the short field technique. I held the brakes, pushed the throttle full forward, and pulled the tail wheel off at only 45 mph. The rising shoreline bank forced me toward the water. Just above stall speed, I lifted off the main gear, flying level above the cold waves—and holding my breath until the plane gained a safe margin of altitude.

It wasn't long before I recognized the military installation of Cape Lisburne. Uncertain about clearance regulations, I swung out over the water and around the rocky, windy cape, picking up a welcome 30 mph tailwind from the cloud-strewn sky. In this unpredictable north, I never knew what to expect: head winds, tail winds, smooth air, or blizzards.

With Point Hope on the narrow spit in front of me, I was now in semi-familiar territory and expected to see familiar faces when I landed. "Hey, Doc, what are you doing up here?" asked my good friend, Leonard Lane, with whom I had gone polar bear hunting. After coming from Barrow, I was impressed by the warmth of this village untouched by the tourist trade. The villagers shook our hands, inquired as to our trip through the bad weather, and filled our stomachs with food and the plane with gas. I wanted to stay on schedule and since I never knew how long the flying weather would last, I hastened to get back into the air.

Even though I'd followed this same route before, Alaska showed me new sights. Between Cape Thompson and Kivilina, we were entertained by seal and buluga whale cavorting in the water, and long ivory-tusked walrus, which the storm had apparently dumped on the shore.

We were making great progress and before long I lowered full flaps and tried to settle on the middle of the runway at Kotzebue. "Doc, what are you trying to do?" asked Mel.

Everytime I taxied more than a few miles per hour, the

plane rose like a kite back into the air. I couldn't figure out what I was doing wrong. Then I remembered the FAA radio report of 25 to 35 mph winds on the runway. Upon releasing the flaps, the plane settled down into normal behavior. "I told you planes naturally fly," I responded.

We only stayed on the ground long enough to refuel and catch a FAA weather report. "What's the good news?" asked Mel.

"Yesterday, a storm chased us and today, we're chasing a storm," I replied. "Let's see how far we can get."

We began our hop-skip-jump back to Tanana through rain showers. Kobuk River. Hog River. By this time, the showers beat down on us in a steady rain and forced us to crawl along at less than 500 feet. "Hughes is probably around the river bend," said Mel. "Let's set down and see if Mr. and Mrs. James are there, and we can check in for a coffee break and get the most recent weather report."

The James's served us hot drinks as I paced around their cabin trying to figure out what to do. We were close to home, only 90 miles away, yet two pilots had tried to get through shortly before we arrived and were forced back. I felt confident, nonetheless, that I could make it through. This was familiar territory, and I counted on the 800-foot pass to be open with a 1,200- to 1,400-foot ceiling. Besides, we could always turn back if we needed to. "Mel, let's refuel and take it on in."

We skirted the south edge of Indian mountain and the plane moved in among the eastward hills. All we needed was one pass that would take us to the west headwaters of the Tozi River. We picked our way into the passes, then fumbled around as thick clouds met us in canyon after canyon. "I'm afraid we're going to have to head back to Hughes." I finally gave in to my frustration.

I turned the plane around and worked my way backward. To my dismay, we were entangled in the labyrinth of green hills and shallow canyons. In and out and around we flew for nearly an hour. Everything looked the same. "Let's face it, Mel," I said, "we're lost, and there's no place to sit down in this terrain."

"Yep, it's a mighty tight spot, Doc." said Mel.

I decided this would be a good time to call on my Almighty Co-pilot, so after a short prayer, I pulled my thoughts together and anaylzed our plight. Our plane compass showed 330 degrees, and it should have read 90 degrees. Something was wrong. Then I realized my foolishness. All this time I'd been relying on only my own sense of direction, when I could have used my radio. Upon tuning into Bettles with the Bendix loop, an old World War II navigational direction finder, I learned that the compass was correct, and that we were heading north to Bettles, rather than south to Tanana.

"Mel, now that we have our directions straight, I think we're going to have to use common sense to get ourselves out of this maze," I said. "I'm going to follow the first stream I find." He didn't seem to be listening, but stared intently past me and out my window.

"Hey, isn't that the burn area we saw the first day of our trip?" he exclaimed.

I looked outside at the blackened hillside. "Sure enough. We must be on the northern slope of the Ray Mountains."

More good news. As we had been searching the ground for clues, the ceiling had lifted in spots to 2,500 feet. Just ahead, I saw what appeared to be a shallow pass, with a slight 100-foot clearance. I squeezed through the gap. Now my problem was to get through the 4,500- to 5,000-foot Ray Mountains. Ragged white clouds covered the peaks.

The Bettles radio helped me decide what to do. "Tanana has 2,500-foot ceiling, wind 20 knots from the south." From this information, I knew that the south wind was pushing and bunching the clouds against the south side of the Ray Mountains. I had read that at times, beneath these conditions, the wind would push a hole up through the clouds. "I'm going to try to find a hole along the northside of the peaks," I told Mel.

Suddenly, through a small gap, I caught a glimpse of the valley on the other side of the mountain. "Here we go," I said. I cut the throttle and began slipping the plane down the hole to the valley. The plane gained speed as rapidly lost altitude. Within minutes, we burst out under the 2,500-foot cloud layer. "We made it!" I shouted. "We're nearly home."

Before we landed at Tanana, I thought of how this unpredictable and rugged land showed no favors to the weak or fainthearted. I loved Alaska, and in moments like this, after conquering its grasp, I wondered why I was leaving its challenge and beauty.

"Say, Doc," said Mel, as though he was reading my thoughts. "This is your last great adventure before heading out to Montana."

"Yep, I'll really pack away the gear now. The barge comes in about a month to transport all our things to Fairbanks, and then a truck will haul it down to the Blackfoot Indian Reservation at Browning."

"What do you think about the doc who's replacing you?" Mel continued.

"He's pretty young, just finished his internship in Kentucky, but seems level-headed." I said. "I hear he's married and has a small child—expects to stay only a year."

We flew in silence. My eyes and mind tried to pack away some of these last images of the good ol' Yukon River and the familiar village, which clung to its banks. The green-roofed FAA station complex came into view, followed by the red-roofed medical facilities. Washing machines on back porches. Children playing on Back Street. Dogs on top of their houses. Gravel pit. Overgrown cemetery. A fishwheel sweeping up unsuspecting fish.

I brought the plane around and placed it gently on the airstrip behind the hospital. Coming to a stop toward the east end, a curious moose stepped out of the woods, turning its massive head strangely to one side, as if to repeat, "Why are you leaving this country you love?"

Anaktuvuk Pass - April, 1959.

Anaktuvuk Pass - April, 1959.

April dog sled races - April, 1959.

Christmas pot lache.

Typical eskimo log cabin at Hungry - November, 1956.

Bringing home the moose - January, 1957.

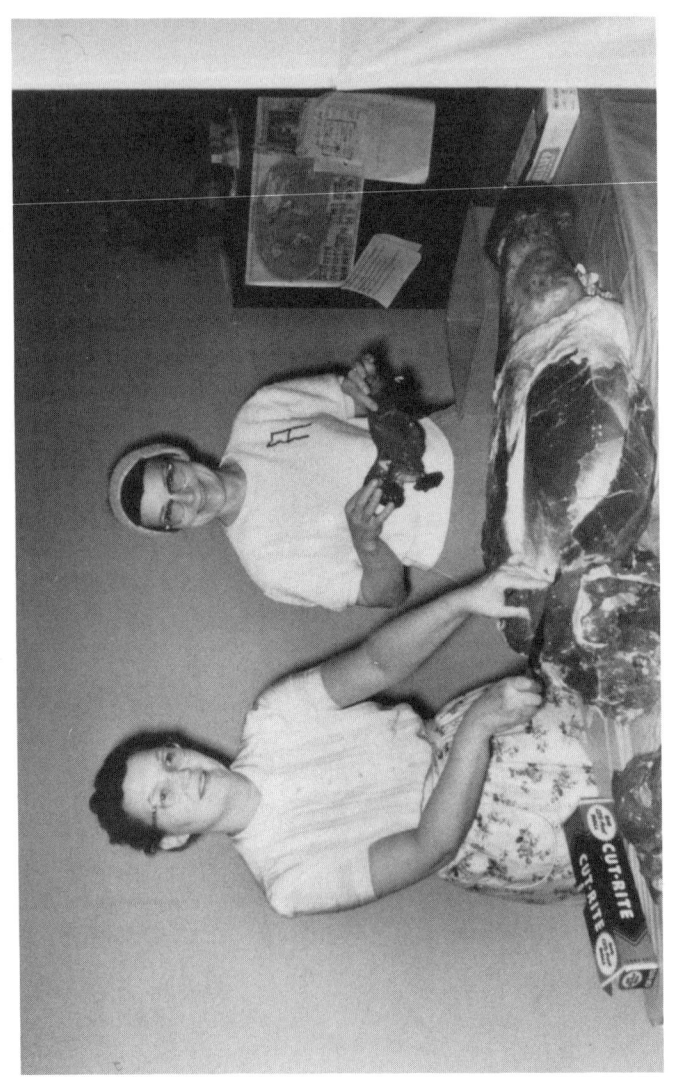

Ruby and Irene cutting up the moose - November, 1956.

Kotzebue Hospital - January, 1956.

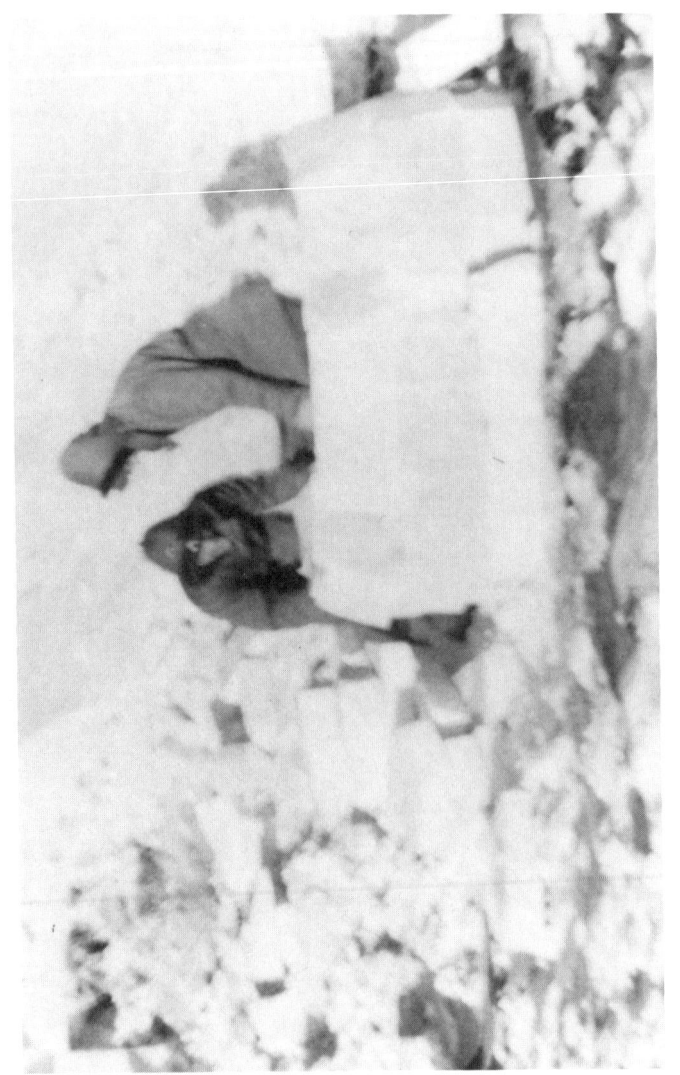

Snowhouse - February, 1958.

Me and the polar bear - March, 1958.

Pulling the whale flipper home at Pt. Hope - March, 1958.

Ice cracks over which our plane skimmed - March, 1958.

Ocean ice flows west of Pt. Hope - March, 1958.

Fish wheel on the Yukon River - July, 1958.

Fish drying racks - July, 1958.

Fairly new log cabin in Tanana - July, 1957.

Tower House and MK buildings at Tanana - March, 1957.

Episcopal Church at Tanana - March, 1957.

At Elmer's - Tanana, Alaska.

Tanana Post Office - March, 1957.

Seward Earthquake/Tidal Wave damage - 1964.

Demolished home in Seward after earthquake/tidal wave - May, 1964.

Peeling logs - December, 1964.

Unloading hay by our barn - August, 1967.

19
Back home
July 1961 to February 19, 1962

Wilbur Hett, Hillsboro, Kansas
Dear Wilbur Hett,
    It's been a long time since I've written you in Hillsboro, Kansas. While I'm spending the night at our medical clinic, keeping an eye on a set of three-pound twins born at midnight, I'll give you a run-down of what I'm doing.
    Last summer we returned to Alaska. After working nine months at the Public Health hosptial on a Blackfoot Indian Reservation in Browning, Montana, we moved on to Tulare, California, where I completed a year of general-practice medical residency at a county hospital. It was a great year for all of us since my parents, brother, sister, and their families lived a short distance away, at Reedley and Fresno. Our children, who have been away from grandparents and cousins, thrived on the

constant "family reunions," which included watermelon feasts, picnics, swimming, and trips up to see giant redwoods. Even though California had mild weather, friends and relatives, and lots of fresh fruit, I was still restless there. It seemed that I'd left my heart in Alaska. A medical journal advertisement, placed by Dr. Paul Isaak, sole physician in the Soldotna area, requested help with his growing practice. I inquired and waited for an answer. In fact, our whole family anticipated Dr. Isaak's reply. Naomi, our oldest child (age 10), found the letter in the mailbox, ran into the house, and jumped up and down as I read it. "Looks like we'll be heading back up to Alaska," I told the family members, who had all gathered around. Even Mishal, (age 3) clapped her hands. (Our other children are Ruth, age 9, and Mark, age 5.)

I had become acquainted with the Kenai Peninsula when we lived in Anchorage and I took floatplane lessons. I'd flown over the Swanson River oil discovery well here on the Peninsula during my practice time. I understand that there is enough gas in our nearby wells to supply all of Alaska. Our oil wells produce 30,000 gallons per day. An oil refinery is being built this spring, north of Kenai.

One reason we chose the Kenai Peninsula is that it has the most rapid growth with the best future development potential in Alaska. The hub of activities seems to be Soldotna, where we are now living. Between 6,000 and 8,000 people are scattered over a twenty-five-mile radius from Soldotna. There is no accurate count since many homesteads are far from roads. The economy is based on oil production and commercial salmon fishing. Our one main grocery store, Wilson's, still extends credit for some people who can only pay for groceries after fishing season.

We are living in a small two-bedroom house where Dr. Isaak previously held his clinic. (He lived in a trailer beside this house-clinic with his wife and five children.) He used the cramped bathroom for a laboratory and had an X-ray machine in one of the bedrooms. The Soldotna airstrip runs through town and behind our house, making it convenient to park the plane, and also to fly to the hospital at Seward. The grocery store is next door.

Dr. Isaak and I are the only physicians in a sixty-five-mile radius. Several local businessmen built the two-story, concrete block medical clinic where we practice now, and which also houses the library and a dentist's office. The clinic is fairly complete and has an excellent X-ray unit, laboratory, minor surgery, and delivery room. There is also a ramp on the side of the building for stretcher cases. Much of the usual hospital work has to be done in our clinic since the nearest hospital is 98 miles away by road, or 65 air miles. Therefore, we do almost all obstetric deliveries and minor surgeries, including tonsilectomies and adenoidectomies here.

In addition to our local medical work, we hold a weekly medical clinic at Seldovia, about 110 miles south of here, where there are no available medical services or any roads. Planes are a must in our work.

Here is some idea of my work routine. Saturday noon, Ruby and I flew over to Nondalton, 180 miles southwest across the Cook Inlet and through the Alaskan Range. We visited with the Arctic Missions missionaries and the schoolteachers, and did physical examinations on all the school children.

Monday, we flew home and I was back in the clinic by 3:00 P.M. My second patient presented himself with abdominal pain. After complete evaluation, Dr. Isaak and I decided he must have immediate surgery for acute appendicitis. The patient was taken by private car to Seward General Hospital and since it was dark and the weather was not suitable for flying, Dr. Isaak and I also drove the 98 icy miles.

Tuesday, we treated 46 patients.

Wednesday, at 8:00 A.M., we took Dr. Isaak's plane and flew to Seward, where we did two surgeries. We returned at 3:00 P.M. and worked in our clinic until 6:30 P.M.

Thursday was a routine clinic day and we had one obstetrical delivery.

Friday was clinic day at Seldovia. It was my turn and I left at 8:30 A.M. I flew across the wooded country and over 18 miles of water to the fishing village of about 400 people. Most of the people are Indians, who earn their living from the local salmon and king crab industries. I offered rides home to two live king crabs. They were over three feet in diameter and crawling all around in my back seat like giant spiders. I stuck them in the bathtub when I got home for the children to see. I finished clinic at 6:00 P.M. and flew back in the bright moonlight. I could see nearly 70 miles.

Saturday morning, I flew Naomi to the nearest orthodontist, at Palmer, which is about 110 air miles away and on the other side of Anchorage. After buzzing the dental clinic, the doctor's wife came to the airfield and took us to their clinic. By noon, we were back in Soldotna.

I am involved in a number of community project committees. Ours is a busy and rewarding life in a truly frontier country. We hope to see some Kansas "tourists" every year, so plan on . . ."

I'd come across a copy of this letter as I was sorting through a stack of papers on my desk. Over the years, I had tried to save letters and newspaper clippings that described my life in Alaska. Who was to know, maybe some day I'd compile all this information into a book.

Rereading this letter made me recall what had taken place since that letter had been written. For one thing, I'd been pushed into veterinary medicine. One routine day at the clinic, I was notified that one of my "patients" was tied to the guardrail on the emergency ramp beside the clinic.

"Dr. Gaede, there isn't a vet in this area, and I thought maybe you could look at my horse," requested a young woman in her late 20s, pulling her plaid wool jacket around her.

I walked out the back door, hoping my farming background would augment my knowledge of medicine. My diagnosis of the problem was an infected barbed wire cut, for which I prescribed antibiotics and an ointment.

Another time, I walked into the waiting room and discovered that my next patient was a spider monkey. The other people patients didn't seem to mind the entertainment, and I suspect that it temporarily alleviated their waiting-for-the-doctor anxiety. The monkey's owner, a woman with three small children who were all crying, quickly explained that the inquisitive creature had swallowed a fishhook. I was well acquainted with fishhook cases. Over the summer both experienced and novice fisher men and women accidentally became fishers of people, rather than fishers of fish. This, however, was the first case when the hook was in the throat.

I took the family members and the family pet into the operating room. "Jeanie, bring me a pillowcase," I told my nurse.

I placed the monkey in the pillowcase, tied shut the open end, and began dripping ether on the cloth over the monkey's head.

The children, who had been silent during this unusual procedure, again started their crying about their favorite pet dying. "The monkey will be fine," I assured them. "Soon he will fall asleep so I can remove the hook from his throat."

After a few moments, my patient stopped thrashing around, and using a long forceps I removed the hook. Almost immediately, the monkey awakened from his short nap, and within minutes he was jumping around the room, chased by the children. I'd been known to tell Ruby that my day at the clinic had been like a zoo, but today I was really telling the truth!

I also practiced medicine on our pet cats, which Ruth and Mishal seemed to collect. In an attempt to control this prolific population, I neutered the cats. Ruby assisted me in these afterwork surgeries. The surgeries required anesthesia, which I routinely administered when I assisted Dr. Isaak when he performed surgery on people. Cats differed from people, however, and I had more difficulty calculating the amount of medication needed. Nothing was more exasperating than to be halfway through surgery and have a cat jump off the operating table.

I remembered in particular the situation with Yofee, Ruth's cat. I was determined that this cat would not interrupt my surgical endeavors. Ruby and I managed to hold down the calico cat, while I administered the anesthesia. Surgery went well and Yofee remained asleep. "O.k., Ruby, let me undo the IVs and let's go home." I said, removing the needle. Much to my dismay, I realized that the intravenous needle had become dislodged and some of the anesthesia had escaped into the muscle tissue. I'd overdosed the cat. Carrying the motionless, yet still breathing, cat in an apple box out to the car, I matter-of-factly said to Ruby, "I do the surgery. You deal with recovery."

As soon as we got home, Ruby placed the cat and the box on the floor by the window and assessed the situation. The cat's eyes were semi-open. She attempted to close the eyes, then resorted to covering them with a moist cloth. Her next concern was dehydration. She threaded a tube down Yofee's throat and poured down eggnog. Her intensive care vigil continued off and on through the night, and the next night, and the next night.

I remained unconcerned. I knew that if anyone could revive the cat, Ruby could. After all, she was the only "nurse" I could get to come out for middle of the night deliveries at the clinic;

and she capably assisted me with roadside car accidents. At other times, she kept patients in our home for postoperation or post delivery care.

One week later, Ruby and I were enjoying an early morning breakfast of sourdough pancakes and moose sausage. Yofee passively joined us in her nearby convalescent box. "Elmer, the cat is doing something," Ruby said, as she noticed that the cat was exhibiting the initial reflex response of swallowing—and about to swallow the food tube. "Yofee is coming back!" she exclaimed. This marked the beginning of Yofee's second of nine lives.

Ruth wondered how Yofee would act after her lengthy voyage into the unknown. Truthfully, Yofee was not one of our more intelligent cats, and we noticed no difference in her behavior.

These animal stories were fun to tell guests around the Sunday dinner table, but the essence of life on the Peninsula entailed hard work. We were one of the last families to get in on the Homestead Act. We "proved up" a flat, heavily wooded 80 acres on Gas Well Road, about three miles west of the Soldotna bridge.

The first time we walked about this parcel, a bearded old-timer, carrying a large pistol on his belt, stalked out of the woods. The gruff man wore rugged army clothes and was over six feet tall. "Who are you and what are you doing here?" he barked out the words.

I answered his questions, but my answer did not seem to please him. He shook his fist and muttered something about us just trying to get this land. Although he was most intimidating, we did not have any trouble with him once we bought the land.

Unlike some homesteaders, we were fortunate to have immediate access to electricity. Another plus was the water table, only 13 feet below the surface. We easily dug by hand through the sandy soil to drive the well points. Then, too, the Gas Well Road was a good gravel road, which could seem insignificant to a newcomer, but a gravel road versus a dirt road made the difference between walking a mile or two during spring "break up" and driving out.

We were given 3 years to "prove up" the homestead, which specified clearing one-eighth of the land and planting an annual crop. Eighty-foot spruce stretched toward the sky with spongy green moss and cranberry bushes gathered at their feet. Golden aspen filled in the space between. Ruby and I cleared 14 acres by chainsaw and axe, cutting wedges in these immense trees, then slowly pushing them off balance until they crashed down into the quiet forest. The laborious process moved slowly over the days and nights of 2½ years. After cutting down several trees, we would trim off the branches and start an enormous bonfire to clean up the debris.

Although our main house was a bi-level with brown stained siding, we peeled some of the straightest trees to build a shiny, varnished log cabin and red tin-roofed horse barn, complete with hay loft. To further enable our homestead construction, we used a portable sawmill and cut between 30,000 and 40,000 board feet of rough hewn lumber, which we used to build a hangar and woodsheds. We worked on my day off and Saturdays, often by moonlight and the light of the bonfires.

At times we managed to capture the children's energy and direct it into peeling the logs, but usually they played away their natural energy resources by following the leader and walking heel-toe around the wonderful pathway maze of long, fallen logs. From the air, our clearing looked much like a giant game of pick-up sticks.

After our hands-on work, a D8 Cat pulled out the stumps and leveled the land. The stumps were shoved into piles, along with the rich black topsoil that clung to their roots. These stump piles could be seen along all the Peninsula back roads and cleared areas. A number of people owned horses and tethered their horses to the piles where the rich soil, produced lush green grass. Bright pink fireweed and purple-blue lupines thrived amongst the tall grassy stalks.

This work was not only to meet requirements, but for a specific purpose. When all brush and timber was cleared away, we had a ½-mile-long-by-150-feet-wide runway a half-block behind our house. Our herculean accomplishment showed up on aviation charts as the "Gaede private."

In further compliance with the homestead requirements, we planted annual crops of timothy hay and oats on this airstrip. Someone has said, "You can take the boy off the farm, but you can't take the farm out of the boy." My farming instincts sprang forth, and before I knew it, I'd purchased a small Ford tractor for harvesting.

Harvesting was a family project of cutting the hay, then

raking it up and pitching it on a wagon. Although it would seem we had a large field, Molasses, our brownish-black mare, could never have survived the winter on such scanty rations. We ended up supplementing our hayloft with other folk's hay.

Homesteading was a new chapter in our short Alaskan history, but the challenge of mixing medicine with flying remained much the same as it had been in Tanana. During some weeks, Dr. Isaak and I would make several trips to the Seward hospital in his Piper Pacer or 180, or my Family Cruiser.

Seward, a year-around seaport town on Resurrection Bay, curved around many docks as it was nearly pushed into the bay by the mountains. "Resurrection" seemed to be a strange name for the bay, the river flowing into the bay, and the pass through the mountains into the town. Once I had heard the story of its naming it made more sense. Apparently, Alexander Baranof, a Russian fur trader and explorer, met rough seas on his voyage between Kodiak to Yakutat. Unexpectedly, he discovered shelter in this bay and because it was the Russian Sunday of the Resurrection, he named nearly everything *resurrection*.

In spite of Baranof's influence and profuse namings, Seward bore the name of the man who was instrumental in purchasing Alaska from Russia in 1867, U.S. Secretary of State William H. Seward. Fortunately, this frontier town didn't carry the original nickname of the Alaskan purchase, "Seward's Folly" or "Seward's Ice Box."

We pilots had names other than "Resurrection" for the pass that capriciously allowed access to Seward. Often, severe weather brewed in Resurrection Pass and fog clogged our only airway between Soldotna and Seward. Added to these unwholesome conditions, tremendous wind swept along the Anchorage Highway into Seward, nearly blowing cars off the road and creating severe turbulence.

One flight for life to Seward particularly stuck out in my mind. On that particular late summer day, Dr. Isaak and I had been busy with our routine of unroutine activities, such as delivering babies between checking ears and throats of other patients, casting fractured legs and arms, prescribing antibiotics for various infections, and tranquilizing dogs and extracting porcupine quills. Moving at top speed around the clinic, I grabbed the next medical chart: Sherron Justice, twelve years old.

Sherron's mother filled me in with the details. The girl hadn't felt well the previous night and had developed a low-grade fever, nausea, and vomiting. Along with these symptoms, she had right lower abdominal pains. After examining her and doing some blood work in the lab, my suspicions were confirmed. I decided that she had acute appendicitis and would need immediate surgery. I notified Dr. Isaak of the situation, called the Seward hospital to expect our arrival in 90 minutes, and asked the receptionist to reschedule the rest of our day's appointments.

The four of us—Sherron, her mother, Dr. Isaak and myself—walked out to the gravel clinic parking and climbed into Dr. Isaak's Mercedes. Instead of taking the main road through town, we short-cutted across the back streets, crossing over the old airstrip and catching the main road in front of the old clinic-house. The recently completed Soldotna Airfield, lay across the Kenai River and several miles out of town.

The weather looked great from where we stood, some high furoughs of clouds in the calm skies. We never knew what waited for us between here and Seward, but after checking the weather report and fueling my Family Cruiser, we all found our spots in the plane. Dr. Isaak had logged pages of hours and sat beside me as co-pilot. Mother and daughter sat behind us, neither looking too comfortable. I confidently went through the takeoff checklist, opening the throttle and checking the magnetos. Everything sounded fine. Within moments we were airborne.

Dr. Isaak and I never tired of the scenery on trips to and from Seward. First we flew over Skilak Lake, a nearly 16-mile-long, glacier-fed turquoise lake. As pilots and hunters, we always looked for a place to set down in case of emergency—and wildlife. "There's a nice one, Elmer," said Dr. Isaak, pointing out the window to a moose in the marshy shoreline. As we climbed upward into the mountains, we neared Upper Russian Lake, now keeping our eyes open for sheep and goat in the crags, and black bear eating blueberries on the mountainsides. I glanced back at my passenger and patient. The girl slumped toward her mother, unaware of the prospective wildlife tour outside her window.

Just past the lake, I noticed my engine RPM was dropping slowly. I suspected carburetor icing and casually applied carburetor heat. No change. The needle gradually slid around from 2,300 to 2,100 to 2,000, indicating that the engine was slowing down and that the propellor was making fewer rotations. As the mountains ascended, I descended to 800 feet above the thick spruce trees. During the past several years, several planes had crashed in this area because there were no emergency landing areas.

I turned to my veteran co-pilot. "Paul, I'm losing engine power. I'm sure it's carburetor icing, but my carb heat isn't doing any good. Any suggestions?"

Dr. Isaak shook his head. The trees reached upward with only a 500-foot clearance. If we crashed, we'd all have a medical emergency—and not enough doctors to go around. Then, a thought popped into my head . . . something I'd read about carburetor icing: when the carburetor heat didn't remove the ice, lean out the fuel mixture. The engine will run rough since it won't have a balance of oxygen and fuel. Do for a few seconds and shake out the ice. My hands shook as I reached for the smooth red knob. I drew back. I'd lose even more RPM if I leaned the mixture.

When I looked down, I couldn't believe that Alaska had such giant trees—what were they doing up here so close to us?

I had no choice. I firmly turned the red knob. The plane shuttered. "Come on," I heard myself say in a hoarse whisper. Seconds passed. Abruptly the engine sounded different. With a roar of full power, we defied gravity and put 5,000 feet between us and the greenery below. For the moment, I felt relieved; nevertheless, I stopped looking for wild game and concentrated on the gauges and the sound of the engine. After awhile, I adjusted the mixture to its previous setting and pushed in the carburetor heat. My patient was certainly getting more than the daily recommended dosage of excitement today.

During the rest of the trip, the plane reverted back to the slowed RPM and I repeated the process of leaning out the mixture. Even though I knew what worked to keep us in the air, it was a nerve-wracking experience for all of us. Once we landed in Seward, we eagerly thrust our shaky-kneed legs out of the plane and onto the solid ground.

A car from the hospital met us at the airstrip. I helped Sherron and her mother to the car. Surgery went well and we removed a "hot" appendix, which probably would have ruptured if we had waited much longer.

Two hours later, Dr. Isaak and I returned to the airfield, while our two passengers remained at Seward.

The plane soared into the air and climbed out over Resurrection Bay, before turning and swiftly making its way up through Resurrection Pass. As we flew back, high over the treetops, I could almost hear a voice in my past saying, "Mixing flying with medicine sure brought on some excitement for you today. Yes, Mary Ann," I wanted to say. "Some things haven't changed."

I looked over to Dr. Isaak, "Paul, this trip seems to have given you a few more gray hairs."

Not to be outdone, he replied. "Hey, I noticed you look a little gray around the edges, too."

I've earned them all, I thought, and I've probably got a few more coming.

20
The day the earth broke apart
March 1964

There were no pressing medical needs on this Good Friday holiday, so Dr. Isaak and I decided not to hold clinic. Instead, I was working in the back woods of my homestead cleaning up fallen timber and digging trenches to divert water away from the house.

This was an awkward time of year with old, dirty snow mixed with sand and gravel and no sign of fresh greenness. As the days started earlier, we enjoyed broad daylight by 7:00 A.M. The new warmth of 35° to 40° F hinted of relief from winter's cold and darkness, and the snow melted into daytime slush and nighttime ice. The combination of daytime warmth and overnight lows of 5° to 10° F, degrees, however; kept the ground in confusion. Consequently, the snow would melt during the day, but the still-frozen ground did not allow the snow's subsequent runoff to drain properly. Small lakes formed around the house, and the road became a kind of water canal. Homesteaders who did not have gravel roads would abandon attempts at driving in and out to their houses; instead they would park their vehicles by a main road and walk the distance to and from. Dr. Isaak had such a situation. His family would walk a mile back and forth to catch the school bus, to haul in groceries, and so on.

"Elmer!" I looked up and saw Ruby coming toward me, trying to walk around the waterways in her black knee-high rubber boots. "One of your O.B. cases is on the phone."

"I'll be right in," I called back, chopping away at one more chunk of ice before turning toward the house.

Within a few minutes, Mrs. Smith gave me an experienced progress report on her condition. This was not her first baby, so without hesitation I told her I'd meet her at the clinic at about 5:15 P.M. Since we didn't have a hospital, we had all obstetrical deliveries in the clinic. I'd have to find a nurse to assist me.

I changed my heavy work clothes and headed out the door to my VW microbus. "If this is the real thing, I won't be back for supper," I called to Ruby.

I slid along the water-on-ice homestead road, out to the main road, and down to the bridge that spanned the silty Kenai River. The bridge was the only one crossing the Kenai River and connected the lower Kenai Peninsula towns with the main part of the Peninsula. I drove through Soldotna, which spread itself out about a mile east from the bridge down to the Y, where the road came in from Anchorage, and then about another mile north past the clinic and toward Kenai. The town was not large, just spread apart. No one ever walked from one store to another, since in independent Alaskan fashion the stores stood apart a half block or more.

Mrs. Smith met me in the clinic parking lot and took her muddy boots off at the door before walking back to the examining room. "It's a mess out there, isn't it?" she said. "I didn't plan on having a baby at breakup when the homestead roads are so bad."

She lay down on the examining table, which would most likely turn into a delivery table. I began my evaluation. Blood pressure normal; fetal heart rate normal. The baby's head was low. I needed to call a nurse right away. Then, suddenly the room seemed to sway. I reached out to the table to steady myself. How strange, I thought. Was I dizzy? I sat down on the tall stool at the end of the table. The movement continued, now with a distant rumble. I looked up at Mrs. Smith. Our puzzled eyes met and then together we shouted, "Earthquake!"

"Let's get out of here!" I said, helping her off the table. I held on to her arm as we careened down the hall to the emergency ramp door.

The shaking intensified. As we stood looking out the door, I saw the tall spruce and aspen trees whipping violently back and forth until their tops nearly touched the ground. Like the sound of a surf, the roaring became deafening. The post office near us came alive and gyrated on the convulsing ground. Cars lurched crazily on the road as the ground heaved up and down like ocean waves. I'd been in earthquakes at Tanana, but never anything like this.

A jagged crack appeared in the highway in front of a car. The ground opened up about a foot wide and then suddenly clapped shut. As the earth stretched apart and other cracks appeared, the smell of sulfur filled the air. I was spellbound and terrified. The roaring continued and the ground groaned in agony. Will it never end? I asked myself. How long can this last before everything is broken apart?

After four never-ending minutes, the nightmare ended—or so I thought. Silence. "I'm going home," said Mrs. Smith in a shaky voice. "I don't want to have my baby right now." She walked back into the clinic to get her boots and then walked out the front door to her car and drove off.

I walked back into my office. The large clock on the wall, now hanging crookedly, had stopped at 5:36. I pushed back the furniture in the waiting room, which had danced out of place, then called Ruby. The phone was dead. I had to get home.

Just as I opened the front door to walk out, a police officer burst in. "Doc, you've got to stay here to care for any emergencies that might come." I felt pulled between my medical obligations and my concern as a father and husband.

Later Ruby told me of her experience. The ground had groaned and cracked, letting out swamp gas from the shallow fields beneath our homestead. She, too, had tried to call me, but when she picked up the phone all she heard was a woman screaming hysterically on our party line.

In our lab, I found a battery radio to hear about possible damage in other areas. I was suprised to find that many stations were no longer on the air, and I began to wonder if anyone was "out there" or if we were completely alone, and if damage in some areas, such as Anchorage, was so complete that no one remained.

Finally I tuned into a Seattle station, where I gradually learned what had happened in Anchorage. The announcer's reports were so graphic and grim that they sent chills down my back: houses and people swallowed up, bridges destroyed, and fires. The broadcasts were without music and commercials: There was no lightheartedness to break the tension. The extent of the damage in Alaska had only begun to be assessed.

The Good Friday sun slipped away, edging the pink wisps of clouds with gold against the darkening sky. Darkness closed around us. Hour by hour, the night grew blacker and the reports became worse. Aftershocks added to my trepidation. For many people, the nightmare was not over.

A new report informed us that the nightmare was not over for us either—the earthquake had churned up a tidal wave. Our homestead was three miles from the beach and even at that, we were very close to sea level. After such a gigantic quake, which I learned later was of 8.4 magnitude, it was possible that water could come rolling in. Between patients who came and went during the night, I kept my ear to the radio, prayed, and waited for the darkness to break into daylight.

The next day I drove home. This was not the same town I'd driven through yesterday. Signs lay crumpled on the ground, buildings showed slits down their sides, and streets were cracked. I was glad to see that the bridge across the Kenai River was still intact—unlike many of the others. We learned that bridges were out and roads were closed between Anchorage and the Kenai Peninsula.

An old log cabin was the only building not condemned by Civil Defense in the Portage area, a flat area in Turnagain Arm around which the road from the Peninsula to Anchorage wound. About 40 residents had spent the night on high ground above Portage and were evacuated by helicopters. Army engineers cut through snow and rock slides and needed to either rebuild or lay temporary bridges in thirteen areas just to get to Portage, much less the entire distance to Soldotna. As was expected, people rushed to the several grocery stores, where many of the items had been shaken from the shelves and lay in a mess in the aisles.

Unlike the coastal towns, Soldotna itself was in good shape. There was no major structural damage, and because there was no city sewer or water, no main lines were broken. We soon heard cargo planes overhead, landing at Kenai with food supplies.

This minimal damage was not the case in towns such as Homer, Kodiak, Seward, Valdez, and Anchorage. At Homer, only 80 miles away, the dock was ripped loose at Homer Spit, and boats littered the remaining waterway. The landtable had dropped nearly six feet, so with high tides coming in only a few weeks, all the buildings near the dock would be flooded. The fragments of dangling dock were no longer useful at the lower elevation.

At Kodiak island, the tidal waves heaped more damage upon earthquake destruction. Most of the boat harbor was gone and boats littered the beaches. Between 650 and 700 people who had been evacuated from other parts of the island were being fed by the Civil Defense agency at the Kodiak Naval Station. Another 20, to 30 people were unaccounted for.

Reports of devastation continued. Most of the residents from Valdez were evacuated. Governor Eagan said of his hometown, "There is no sign that there ever was a dock or boat area. This area has totally disappeared." Fires added to the chaos and 34 people were known to be dead.

The reports of destruction to human life and material loss at Seward and Anchorage were unbelievable. I had to see for myself the bizarre turmoil resulting from the Good Friday Earthquake. But before I could fly over to survey the damage there was Easter to remember.

The church service took on a new meaning as I thought of the 104 or more people killed in the quake and the grieving of those who had lost these loved ones. I hoped they would find spiritual comfort on this day. I also thought of the traditional Easter story, where an earthquake shook the enormous rock away from the entrance of Jesus' tomb. The guards attending this tomb were terrified and confused—and I could certainly understand why.

That afternoon, Dr. Isaak and I flew to Seward to see the terrifying confusion there. Seward was closed to outsiders, but since we were both members of the Civil Air Patrol, in addition to being on the hospital staff, we were granted special permission to enter the area.

It really didn't take much to keep people out of Seward. The road into Seward was badly broken apart, and the main portion of the runway was unusable. The cross runway where we had our hangar was in shambles with heaps of gravel, trees and debris. There was no trace of our hangar.

As if the earthquake hadn't rendered enough damage, a tidal wave had rolled in and crushed everything in its path for about three-quarters of a mile in from the bay. It was a spooky feeling as we surveyed the damage. The mile-long waterfront had collapsed into the ocean bay and docks, warehouses, offices, and storage tanks had vanished. Rails, train cars, and engines were melted together or tossed about as if an angry child had tired of play. It was just as the Anchorage Daily News had reported, "The supply life-line for the interior of Alaska—the Alaska Railroad—will have to be brought back from the near-dead. Its facilities and equipment at Seward are a mass of molten steel and burning railroad cars. Unofficial sources say it will be weeks before the 470-mile line is again in full operation." In a lagoon a half-mile from Seward, two rails dipped up and down with the tide. Wrecked cars, twisted rails, crumbled houses, and fire made what had been just crowned an All American City look like a garbage dump.

The eerie feeling intensified as we flew south of Seward before returning to Soldotna. "Didn't there used to be a mountain peak over there?" asked Dr. Isaak.

"I thought we knew this area like the back of our hand, but something seems different," I answered.

"Do you think an entire mountain could be swallowed up?" he asked.

I didn't answer. That concept was too overwhelming. For some time we flew in silence. After awhile, Dr. Isaak pointed out the window and said, "Look! That lake is empty."

I pushed the stick forward and we flew down for a closer look. "The bottom must have cracked open and swallowed up the water!" I exclaimed.

Even though I'd seen enough for one day, I felt compelled to go to Anchorage and confirm for myself the radio and newspaper reports. I'd heard that the residents were living in a state of emergency, with many streets buckled, water lines broken and power lines snapped. Reportedly, drinking water tanks and field toilets were set up for temporary use. People were being urged to get typhoid shots and not to hoard groceries. One school had split open, and all schools were closed until further notice.

When I managed to get to Anchorage, my first impression of the city was that an enormous plow had cut across the residential area of Turnagain, which overlooked the Knik Arm. The ground had sloughed away and homes and cars had fallen down to the water and into yawning pits. In some spots, the frozen ground was twisted; in other places patches of ground were like puzzle pieces in disarray. Some ground had been raised and othere spots were lowered. Some ground had been stretched apart and needed to be pushed back together.

Between 100 and 125 families had called this area home. I thought of the people I'd heard about who were outside their collapsing homes and had disappeared into the gapping chasms. I flew on. Streets and lawns had been wrenched apart. A multi-storied apartment building lay crumpled. The new, five-story J.C. Penney building had buckled, the walls shearing away and crushing a half-dozen cars parked at the curb. Fifth Avenue was now above the previous floor level of many buildings that had sunk.

I returned to Soldotna with mixed feelings. I was grateful for my family's safety, yet I had a heavy heart for those who had experienced tremendous loss. Buildings could be restored, and the land would eventually heal, but there would be permanent scars in the lives of many people as they remembered the terror of the Good Friday Earthquake.

In my line of work, death and birth accompanied one another. In contrast to the many who had died, I thought of the "Earthquake Baby," who Mrs. Smith did have several days later. The child had truly come into the world at "breakup" when the Alaskan world broke apart.

21
Return to Point Hope
Summer 1982

The wind blew steadily in our faces and our feet stuck to the sand as if it were wet cement. White-capped waves pounded against the beach, sending frothy fingers of water up toward the short grass-tuffed bluff where we trudged, one foot in front of the other. Fog ebbed and flowed around us, teasing us with mirages of people and houses just beyond the next tundra knoll.

This arctic coastline beach was familiar. I'd been downed here twice before: once after the polar bear hunt at Point Hope, and then on my way back from Barrow. Some things didn't change, such as the wind, which meant business and cut right through my layers of insulated jacket, blue plaid flannel shirt, and T-shirt—right to the marrow.

But other things, had changed. As I walked through the thick, blowing mist, Mishal, now a young woman, walked beside me, her long, black curly hair trying to free itself from her lavender knit hat. Beside her, Ruth's husband, Roger, bent his head into the wind, pulling his tan-hooded jacket around his lean body.

Let me digress. Even though Alaska, flying, and my adventures had remained much the same, over the years my children had grown up and either married or left home. Naomi, a writer and speaker, married Bryan Penner, an engineer and private pilot. They lived in Denver, Colorado, with their two children.

Ruth, a homemaker, was married to Roger Rupp, a pilot, flight instructor, and A & P (Airframe and Power Plant) mechanic and authorized inspector. They remained on the homestead and built a house for their three children and a hangar on the other side of the airstrip behind our house. Roger conveniently conducted his business right outside his back door, and the airstrip often had a multicolored lineup of planes. Having Roger nearby was like having my own personal mechanic, and with all my close calls, it was more necessity than luxury.

Just a long stone's throw away and up the airstrip, smoke floated out the chimney of my son Mark's cedar house, which he, his wife Patti, and one daughter called home. Mark had become a computer technician for the oil industry, and Patti was a secretary-bookkeeper. Mark also used the airstrip. Since the time we had returned to Alaska, he was my constant flying buddy, sitting on a rolled-up sleeping bag and peering out the window. In fact, he flew with me so often that flying the J-3 and Cessna 180 came as easily as riding a bicycle for him. He was a natural pilot who, at age 16, soloed. I'll never forget his laugh and a wide grin that day when he had proudly displayed his cut shirttails.

For awhile, Mishal migrated to a Denver art school during the school year, returning home each summer. One day as she read the *Anchorage Times*, her eyes were drawn to a photo of an Eskimo girl from Point Hope who was visiting Sea World in San Diego. Beneath the picture was the girl's name, "Darlene Tooyak." Since I'd told Mishal the name of her birth mother, she knew that the Tooyak girl must be a relative of hers.

This information set in motion a series of events, beginning with contacting the Tooyaks in Point Hope, discovering her birth mother in Denver, and being invited by her relatives to visit Point Hope. The previous year, we had flown to Point Hope, where a reunion took place and she began to learn about her rich heritage.

Now we were again returning to Mishal's village of Point Hope. When we left this July 1st morning, we hadn't intended to take a walking tour of the coastline, nor had I expected to set down another plane on this beach—this time a blue and white Cessna 180.

The day had opened with overcast skies in variegated shades of gray. In addition to Mishal, Roger, and me, our group included my sister, Lillian Pauls, from Reedley, California. As we walked out the door to my hangar, I overheard Ruby tell Lillian, "I hope you have fun. Something exciting usually happens when someone flies on a long trip with Elmer."

We rolled the 180 out of the hanger, climbed in, and taxied out to the homestead airstrip. After checking the area for Ruth's horses, we spun the plane around in front of Roger's hangar and completed the flight checklist. In addition to four passengers, the plane was heavily loaded with "just-in-case" emergency gear. Nevertheless, by the time we passed Mark's house we were airborne and heading north for another adventure.

As we crossed the Cook Inlet, oil platforms stood on their long legs in the deep water. We skirted Anchorage, flying over the small village of Tyonek and bravely making our way to Rainy Pass in the Alaskan Range. All passes collect weather problems since fog, clouds, and snow become stuck in the higher elevations. This situation is intensified by winds, which funnel through the passes. I'd flown through Rainy Pass a number of times, and as I commented to Roger, "Rainy Pass is the one of the trickiest and most dangerous passes I've been through."

Today was no exception. "Seatbelt check," I said over my shoulder. The updrafts threw us up, and everything that was not securely fastened flew around the cabin. All that goes up must come down, and without notice, a downdraft would suck us down. Flying along in this fashion was much like riding a bucking bronco. Light snow met us as we neared the middle of the pass, but didn't hamper our visibility. There was a light at the end of the tunnel and bright sunshine beckoned us over to flatter country.

The flight continued as planned, over winding rivers, above

nameles lakes, across the wide Yukon River, and to a fuel stop at Galena. After awhile, clouds bunched together and escorted us to Kotzebue, where drizzle steadily streaked our windshield. I reached for the radio controls. "I don't mind flying in rain," I said to Roger. "But I don't care to encounter the unwholesome fog along the coastline. I'll see what FAA has to report."

After a few moments, Roger looked at me expectantly. "Well?"

"Kivalina is socked in. We'll have to wait it out here in Kotzebue." Over my shoulder I told Mishal and Lillian, "Time for sightseeing." Then, I put the plane nose down and brought it in for a landing.

Old and new overlapped throughout the village. Caribou racks and skins hung on a house next to a Dairy Queen. A dogsled leaned against a snowmachine. In front of us, a tour bus, lurched to a stop and excited tourists stepped out into the wind and rain, then hopped about trying to avoid the end-to-end puddles. We walked along the muddy streets to the radio station where we would send a free message by tundra radio—Tundra Tom Toms—to Mishal's uncle, Andrew Tooyak, explaining our delay. Along the way, three-wheelers with drivers of all ages careened down the street, splashing water everywhere.

After taking care of business at the radio station, we squeezed in among the tourists at the jade factory. The crude jade was cut from the jade hills to the east along the river, and after seeing the jade jewelry before and after its polishing, we realized we'd walked past enormous boulders of raw jade on our way to town from the airport.

The gray skies lingered above us, and we had time to spare. Mishal knew that her aunt, Viola Norton, lived in Kotzebue, but had never met her. Mishal asked around at the local shops and stores until she was pointed to the residential area only a couple blocks from the beach. At the house door, we stood behind Mishal, as she verified her identity to the hesitant Viola, who kept looking over Mishal's shoulder at the three of us. Finally, after Mishal supplied enough information, Viola invited us inside. Undisturbed by our presence, Viola's two teenagers slept on the floor near us as we visited. (Natives typically stay up nonstop during the long summer days, sleeping only when absolutely tired.)

Even though the conversation flowed along, I kept glancing out the window at the skies, anxious to reach our destination. Before saying goodbye, Viola's husband, Cyrus, took us out to the garage. "Viola and I speared these a few days ago," he said pointing to the heads and tusks of three walruses. "We were up by Kivalina in our fishing boat."

I hoped that by now the fog had cleared out of Kivalina. If we could make it that far, we'd have a good foothold in our trek up to Point Hope. Before taking off, I found a local pilot fueling his plane, and trying to sound casual I asked, "How are the beaches for landing?"

"If they're wet, they're o.k., but if they're dry watch out," he said.

I was ready to try it. After three hours of touring Kotzebue and waiting out the weather, we climbed back into the plane and pushed toward Kivalina. The coastal Eskimo village was clear. We weren't that far from our destination now, but a short distance past this landmark, thick clouds obscured the ground, affording us an infrequent peak at the tundra and lakes below and squelching our hopes. "Dad, check to see if there are any other pilots around," suggested Roger.

I got on the radio and requested a weather report from any pilot who might be flying in the area.

"Point Hope is socked in with fog. I can't find a hole to get down, so I'm turning back," a pilot called back.

"Hey troops, we need to find a hole," I said, recruiting everyone to this task.

Toward the north, Roger spotted one. I flew over to it, spiraled down, and scooted back over the shoreline. I knew the landmarks beneath us and estimated that we were only 15 miles from Point Hope.

As we approached Point Hope's airfield, the fog rapidly crowded us down toward the sand, until our forward visibilty was totally obscured. I made a quick 180-degree turn and backtracked, trying to find the hole we'd come down through. Fog from the open water joined forces with the fog from behind, until there was no place to escape.

"Roger, I'm putting it down," I said. "The beach is wide and smooth, and goes for miles. It looks good enough for a DC 3 to land." Without taking my eyes off the beach, I called back to Lillian and Mishal, "Hang on!"

With first-notch flaps, we slowly settled onto the inviting

sand. To my amazement, the landing was perfectly smooth. Our relief was short-lived, however, as the plane abruptly decelerated. At first, I thought my brakes had locked. Too late, I realized that the sand was soft and looking out my window, I saw the wheels were plowing six-inch furrows. Using full power, I forced the bogging wheels up the bank to higher beach until the plane relinquished its struggle with the sand.

"This is the end of the line for now," I said, opening up the door.

Roger and I scouted out the area for potential firm ground and takeoff strip. At the very top of the beach and several hundred feet away, the sand no longer sunk beneath our feet. Since the plane's engine could not move the plane out of the sand, there was no way we expected to tow it ourselves. Like beach scavengers, we searched for pieces of flat driftwood and scraped water-stained plywood to place under the wheels. Following much huffing and puffing, we pushed the plane along the makeshift track to compacted sand.

I needed to position the plane farther along the beach for our next takeoff and expected that I could just taxi over, now that I had a firmer foundation. Roger, Mishal, and Lillian stood off to the side as I returned to the plane. The engine started easily and the wheels slowly moved along the sand. Then suddenly, my front wheels dropped into a soft spot, a gusty tailwind caught the wings, and the plane tail shot up into the air, forcing the rotating prop into the sand. Immediately, I turned off the ignition, grabbed my tie-down ropes, and climbed out of the awkwardly angled plane, trying to avoid the gas pouring out of the wing tanks.

Roger was already running toward the plane. I lassoed the tail wheel and together we pulled the tail back to the sand. "I guess we'd better check out damage to the prop," I said, not really wanting to see the bad news.

Roger examined the prop, running his fingers along the small two- to three-inch curls at the prop ends. "This plane isn't going anywhere until we can fix this prop," he said.

I broke the news to our small group. "Well, gang, it looks as if the plane will stay here. We can either stay here until someone finds us, or we can walk to the village—since no one knows we're here."

"How far out do you think we are?" asked Mishal.

"I'd guess about eight or nine miles," I said.

A strong wind cut through the dense fog, sending shivers through our bodies and persuading us to find dry shelter. This would not be a leisurely stroll on a sun-kissed beach. Rather, it would be a real nature hike. Instead of a bird's-eye view of this northland, we would get to take in a caribou's eye view. Skeletous parts of whales and caribou littered the beach and we almost stumbled over a dead walrus.

"Lillian, now you can say you're really seen Alaska," I said. "This is certainly off the beaten trail of most tourists."

"I wouldn't mind some California heat right now," she countered.

Three-wheeler tracks encouraged us that civilization was nearby. After awhile, ice and snow on the beach compelled us to walk above the bank on the spongy tundra. At first we talked, but later we saved our energy for walking. Up and down the hummocks we trudged, always straining our eyes for sight of the village. Sea spray fogged up my glasses and eventually seeped through the layers of our clothes. We'd walked for six and a half hours and we all needed to get out of the damp cold in order to maintain our body heat. Surely we had to be at the village soon.

"Look at the abandoned snowmachine!" said Mishal, who was a short distance ahead of me. "And here's a real path."

"Listen. I think I hear fireworks and three-wheelers." added Roger.

We quickened our pace.

"There's the orange runway marker," said Roger.

"The runway is about a mile long," I said to my weary nature hikers. "And the village is only a mile and a half after that. We're going to make it."

We pressed on through the fog. At approximately 3:00 in the morning, we left the tundra and walked into the graveled village of Point Hope. The forty or so prefabricated houses on short stilts all looked the same, except for some variety in the earthtone colors. None of them had names or house numbers, and we weren't sure where Mishal's uncle Andrew lived. Although social calls are usually not made at that hour of the night, we looked around for houses with lights on. We felt like trick-or-treaters knocking on the doors in the eerie cobwebbed fog. No one answered. Lillian and I tried public buildings, and then the abandoned Episcopal church. The door creaked open and we entered the sanctuary, finding much-needed shelter.

Meanwhile, Roger and Mishal had nearly literally run into a pick-up, which was driving around the village. Mishal explained the odd circumstances of their arrival, and the driver took them to Mishal's uncle's house. Before they collapsed and immediately fell asleep, they asked the driver to pick up Lillian and me. That kind good Samaritan searched until he found us and invited us to his house, where we, too, fell asleep.

Brilliant sunshine woke us the next morning, wiping away the fog that had enshrouded the village and seacoast the night before; in the brightness we could see clearly for miles around.

Some things hadn't changed over the years, and the villagers rallied to our need. Enoch Tooyak supplied his fishing boat, in which Roger and I returned to the plane. In preparation for the propeller repairs, Roger took with him a large hammer, pipe wrench, cresent wrench, small anvil, and hack saw. I was grateful for his help in this unexpected predicament.

We reached the shore where the disabled plane waited, and in the sunlight, we could look back across the water at the village, precariously balanced on the spit of land jutting into the ocean. We had been so close, yet so far away as we walked for nearly 13 miles following the curve of the land to the village.

After completely unloading the plane to make it as light as possible and piling everything in to Enoch's boat, Roger worked on the propeller and examined the engine for further damage. During this time, about twelve other Eskimos arrived in fishing boats. Together, we walked the plane to the takeoff area, standing it on its nose yet another time.

"Roger, how would you like the honor of flying the plane to the village? You are about 15 pounds lighter than I am," I said to my near look-alike. "Besides, you've had more flying experience than me."

"No, Dad," he solemnly answered. "It's your plane and I'll let you take the big chance. Use first flaps and get past the first 200 feet, and you'll be light enough to ride the top of the sand."

I started the engine, which purred to my satisfaction. I

taxied a few feet, still listening to the engine, then opened the throttle. Every time I hit an indentation or rise in the sand, I held my breath. The plane eased off the sand and staggered into the air. Rather than short-cut across the water, I followed our pathway around the shoreline to the village. Mishal and Lillian met me when I landed, and Roger returned with Enoch and our plane gear.

We spent the rest of the day exploring the village, which reflected the old and new. In the old village, which had nearly been washed out by fall storms, the sod houses remained semisubmerged in the tundra. Each house had a low, tunnellike entrance, which kept the heat in and the cold out. I could see how in winter, when snow covered these houses, they looked like the igloos many people believed Eskimos to live in.

In another area, we walked around the cemetery, a truly unusual sight since it was fenced in by eight- to ten-foot-tall whale bones. In the last two decades, each village had been given a quota of whales they could attempt to kill. This year, the Point Hope Eskimos had harpooned their allotment of three, but only killed one. We found the grave of Mishal's grandmother, the woman I had taken movies of in my first trip to Point Hope, nearly 24 years ago.

The new homes had attached mini-garages for three-wheelers and snowmachines. Many homes had televisions, which provided a window into all the world for these top-of-the-world people. Permafrost restricted Point Hope's use of a water and sewer system, and the indoor toilets were lined with plastic bags, which required daily disposal. Running water entered each home from an individual tank in the mini-garage.

Before leaving the next day, we took time to attend the services at the Episcopal Church. The congregation heartily sang the hymns and patriotic Fourth of July songs in both English and Eskimo.

Mishal gave hugs and farewells to her relatives, and the four of us climbed back into the plane and retraced our way home. Some things hadn't changed. We left the brown, treeless arctic slope for dark-green spruce-covered hills and mountains, dotted by blue lakes and yellow swamps. We dodged thunderstorms and crossed tangle-up rivers, refueled the plane at Galena, and made our roller-coaster trip through Rainy Pass.

As we came across the Cook Inlet, I looked down. Some

things had changed over the years. Oil platforms greetedg us with blinking lights. Behind me, Mishal's face pressed against the window, and beside me Roger checked the gauges. Change was inevitable, but my life in Alaska was still packed with flying and adventure.

22
Flight by faith
October 1982

The Alaskan sun only teased the 35° F temperatures on this late October day. Carefully I crammed lumber and other building supplies into my Cessna 180 as it patiently waited beside my homestead hangar. I expected a routine flight across the inlet and through the mountains.

My destination, 150 miles west, would lead me across the Cook Inlet, through the Alaskan Mountain Range, and to Lake Clark via the 60-mile Lake Clark Pass. Although the pass was frequently plagued by treacherous weather and although its floor was littered by numerous accidents, I felt confident. After all, I'd flown the Alaskan mountains for over 20 years and navigated through this pass 12 to 15 times each year for the past several years. I figured I could fly it blindfolded. Little did I know that this confidence in myself would soon be tested.

Today FAA weather briefing indicated 2,000-foot broken

clouds with occasional snow squalls at Port Alsworth. The pass was estimated closed to marginal. The pass was often "marginal" yet flyable, so I decided to check it out for myself. With this in mind, I climbed into my plane and took off from my half-mile-long grassy airstrip.

After climbing to 5,000 feet over the Inlet, I called Kenai radio. "This is Cessna 9762 Gulf. Do you have any recent pilot reports through Lake Clark Pass?"

"Cessna 62 Gulf, a Cessna 180 came through from Port Alsworth an hour ago and reported marginal conditions," crackled the reply.

A second voice entered the conversation.

"Cessna 9762 Gulf, call me on 122.9."

Quickly I changed frequencies.

"Doc, this is Jack. I just came through the pass an hour ago. It was marginal, but I made it o.k. It should be improving. I'm on my way back. Do you want to fly it together?"

"Sounds good," I replied.

Like long fingers, gray clouds reached across the 8000-foot-high Alaska Range, ready to snatch planes that dared enter its inner sanctum. When I arrived at the entrance to the pass, the accessible ceiling of 3,500 feet mocked my indecision.

"Doc, I'm about a mile behind you," Jack called over the radio.

"I'll go ahead and give it a try," I replied, accepting the challenge.

A few aspen, stubbornly refusing to relinquish their golden leaves to winter's grasp, speckled the mountain sides and seemed out of place in this dark canyon. Flying several miles into the narrow east end, I turned left. Before me, a glacier crept across the center of the pass, accompanied by snow flurries. From this summit, a river flowed away, both to the east and west. The glacier had a bad reputation. In the winter, it often produced "white-out" conditions which blinded planes—planes later found crashed.

I dropped to only 1,100 feet, gaining an uncomfortably close view of the treacherous blue crevasses, yet able to fly on past the glacier.

Then I was blinded! Quickly I made a 180-degree turn. Enveloped in the snow flurries I groped for direction. My turn-and-bank indicator told me I was not level even though I felt level. Suddenly I realized I was flying vertically alongside the mountain, mistaking it for the floor of the Pass. "Help me," I prayed.

Reorienting myself, I flew back over the glacier, where there was partial visibility. Immediately I checked for carburetor icing and the insidious wing icing, which destroys the lift necessary to carry a plane through the air. "Jack, it's bad in there," I called over the radio. "I've turned back."

"O.k., Doc, I'll punch into it and give you my opinion. I've flown it so many times that I can easily pick out landmarks."

Even with our rotating beacons, navigation lights, and landing lights, I did not see Jack pass me.

"I'm past the glacier and over the lake now," he called after a few minutes. "It's pretty bad, but I can pick out some trees on my left. I think we'll be all right. I'll guide you through. Are you still over the glacier?"

The valley was obscured and the possiblity of losing my way was great. Could I trust Jack? It was true that conditions could improve. On the other hand, the pass threaded between 6,000- to 8,000-foot mountains. But, then, I'd known Jack for over twenty years—he was a good pilot. Deciding to trust him, I answered, "Yes, Jack, I'm still here."

"O.k. Head down the middle of the valley. Watch your compass and stay on that heading—don't turn, no matter how wrong it feels." Jack seemed to know what he was talking about. "Keep your altimeter at 1,200 feet and airspeed at 150 mph."

With no sight of Jack's plane and only a voice to follow, I tracked down the middle of the canyon. "Jack, I'm on the east edge of the lake. I can't see across."

"Doc, you're about a half mile behind me. You'll soon see a row of spruce trees to your left just after you cross the lake. Don't look ahead. Trust your instruments. Trust me."

I had almost no forward visibility, but out my side window I did see the spruce trees lined up and pointing the way.

"O.k. Now you should see a line of trees on your right. Follow them. In another few seconds you'll see the edge of a hill on your right . . . Now make a slight correction with your compass heading to the right—only a few degrees." I clung to Jack's words.

My heart pounded. The landmarks didn't look familiar. Was this the right direction? Maybe I should turn to my left. How had I gotten myself into this? Silently I shouted a prayer, "Oh

God, I made a mistake to enter this valley—will you help me anyway?" I felt wedged in between the snow and the unknown.

My hands, damp inside my warm winter gloves, clung to the stick. Carefully I manuevered the plane. One wrong move and I'd be a statistic in this valley of death.

Time seemed suspended even though the plane fought through the choking blanket of snow at 2½ miles a minute. Clearing my throat and wetting my lips, I radioed Jack. "What now Jack? Are you picking up any ice?"

"Well, Doc, there is some, but not more than a quarter-inch on the wings and struts . . . You should be over the little pond on your right."

"Yes . . . I can see about a quarter mile ahead now. What comes next?" I needed to hear his voice.

"In another minute you'll come to a branch in the river. If you follow what *appears* to be the river it will go to the right. Don't go that way—it's deceiving and leads to a dead-end. Remember the Beaver plane that cracked up in there last year? Instead, look at your compass and keep going straight, over the solid stand of trees. You may not see the river for half a minute, but don't worry—by the way, did you see the big bull moose below you?"

Don't worry? I wiped my forehead and strained my eyes for the river. Finally it appeared.

"Doc, it's looking better ahead," Jack's words kept me going.

Sure enough, within a couple of minutes the snow let up and I could see ahead two miles. "We made it!" I nearly yelled as I unclinched my jaws and relaxed my grip on the stick.

The hours of anxiety dissolved into nine minutes of actual flying time—still long enough to allow for a fatal accident. I sighed a quick prayer, "Thanks God for flying with me in the white-darkness."

As we broke out of the canyon over Lake Clark, Jack indicated his own feelings of relief, "Boy, Doc, that was worse that I've ever been through."

"I don't care to do a repeat on that. Thanks for talking me through, and I'm glad we both made it," I replied.

The rest of the trip to Port Alsworth was in sharp contrast to the previous flight, and as I slowly settled back in my seat, I recalled another close call with death. In the early '70s, I'd volunteered to help Missionary Aviation Repair Center (MARC) shuttle students from the Mission Covenant High

School at Unalakleet back to their village homes during the springtime. I was in my four-place Maule Rocket with a 220-horsepower fuel-injection engine. Between flying in a powerful plane and being familiar with the western Alaska coast, I felt confident.

On that particular day, I'd just dropped off students at Selawik and Kotzebue, and was on my way to Moses Point on Norton Sound. The flight to Moses Point was routine and after learning that no fuel was available, I closed my flight plan and continued on to Nome for gas. One fuel guage indicated plenty of fuel, so I figured I'd have no trouble making it the additional 40 minutes.

As I crossed Golovin Bay, 30 miles toward Nome, the onshore weather deteriorated and clouds obscured the hills. Visibility appeared better over the water, so I swung out about a mile and cruised above the waves at 400 feet. Without warning, the engine quit. Instantly, I turned the plane toward the shore. The bay was in breakup conditions, with many scattered small ice flows. None were larger than 50 feet in diameter—certainly not large enough for an emergency landing. Quickly I set up a glide. I couldn't understand it. My fuel gauge showed one-fourth full. Desperately I switched both fuel tanks "on," pumped the throttle, pushed the electric primer, and in hopes of draining the tanks rocked the wings. No response.

Without power, the 155 mph cruise speed rapidly bled down to 80 mph, and the plane gradually began losing altitude. I estimated that without power, I would be ditching about a half mile from shore. The plane would sink in about three minutes and I'd last about two minutes in the frigid waters—there was no human hope of surviving. My only prospect was an icy grave. The airspeed declined to 60 mph and my altitude was less than 100 feet above the menacing waters. "God, save me! I prayed out loud. The glide continued downward to less than 40 feet. In an attempt to prolong the flight, I pulled first notch of flaps. Touchdown was less than five seconds. Suddenly the engine surged to full power and the plane began to climb. I was shocked and nearly numb with joy. God had heard my prayer and saved my life. Then just as I crossed the shoreline at 200 feet altitude, the engine again quit. This time, however, I was not scared. Snow-covered flat tundra spread out all beneath me, ready for an emergency landing. Just as I had done the first time, I rocked the wings to drain out any possible gas.

The engine caught. I turned inland, located the small Golovin airstrip, and landed.

With shaky knees, I climbed out of the plane. Mr. Olson, the local air service operator, met me and listened to my story. He then offered to gas my plane. I walked around, glad to be alive and on dry land.

"You are very fortunate to have made it here," Mr. Olson said with astonishment. "You used up five of your six unusable gallons of gas."

My fuel gauge had been in error. With God's divine help, I'd been able to slosh enough gas around in the wing tanks and down to the engine.

The sight of Lake Clark brought me back to the present. I started my descent and ended my ponderings about life and death. My relationship to God was one of faith, even though I couldn't see Him and even when I made wrong decisions. He was a constant companion who traveled through life's canyons and over life's rough waters.

23
No ordinary day
March 1984

Just an ordinary Saturday, I thought, as I planned to fly my Cessna 180 from Soldotna to Port Alsworth to work on my house there. The scattered clouds resting against the clear sky offered no hint of the turbulence this extraordinary day, March 3, 1984, would bring to my life. Brisk air greeted me as I strode out the front door in my typical flying gear of flannel shirt, blue jeans, and insulated coveralls. My heavy workboots crunched on the graveled circle drive, certainly a welcome sound after the winterlong crunch of snow.

Instead of going back to my hangar by the taxi-way that extended to the airstrip, I proceeded toward the homestead road in front of the house. The chickens clucked good morning as I walked past their pen. Between the circle of front lawn and the road grew a miniature forest of spruce and birch, which shielded the house from traffic on the road. Rising above the grove, the orange windsock waved gaily in the gentle breeze.

During this breakup season, the homestead airstrip turned into a lake, and therefore the front road served as a temporary landing strip. This morning, four planes, including my newly painted white-and-blue 180, stood at attention like sentries guarding the entrance to our homestead. I'd owned the 180 for nearly three years now, but still found it to be difficult to land properly, since it bounced easily when it touched the ground.

I tossed an extra parka into the back of the plane, where there already was a tent, sleeping bag, and emergency rations. After buckling in, I started the engine, checked for cars on the road, and slowly taxied to the south end of the road. I passed my Super Cub, on the right which was a short distance from Roger's Cessna 172. I spun the plane around before I reached the Gas Well Road and Jones Stub intersection. The neighboring homesteaders had learned to be cautious when enntering this double-duty road.

Except for some gusty winds, it was a perfect day. Adding "watch for cars" to my preflight list, I checked the mags and prepared to take off. The plane, heavily loaded with lumber, accelerated down the "runway" and lifted off, and the ground rapidly dropped away.

I headed to Kenai and then across the Cook Inlet toward Lake Clark Pass. I anticipated getting into Port Alsworth without any weather problems, but shortly after entering the pass, a snowstorm enveloped the plane. I didn't want any repeat adventures in this pass, so I did a 180-degree turn, headed back to blue skies, and called Kenai radio with a report of the actual conditions in the pass. "I'll fly around for half an hour before trying again," I told the weather briefer. I figured my chances were 50-50 I'd have clear sailing within the half hour.

As I flew around, I thought of all the planes with which I'd cut ruts in the Alaskan sky. Prior to this one, I'd had the powerful Maule Rocket, which I nearly ditched into the Norton Sound and which two years ago I did crackup in on the Kenai Peninsula. That had not been a pleasant experience for me or my passenger. I was coming back from a staff meeting at the hospital in Seward and lost power at 400 feet. I pancaked into muskeg and bounced into spruce trees, burying my face into the instrument panel. My passenger, Lee Bowen, the Soldotna pharmacist sustained a broken ankle, and I had a compression fracture of the upper lumbar vertebra. Although I was in good hands with the well-qualified clinic nurses, Dr. Isaak quickly returned from Seward, in his plane, and sutured my face back together. It took over 50 stitches to pull together my forehead, chin, and mouth area. Five teeth were knocked out. Since I couldn't shave over this new "face job" I grew a goatee, mustache, and long sideburns. I knew I had to get back into the air so I wouldn't be overcome by fear. After a month I went up with a friend in his small plane.

But that was two years ago, and right now I had a trip to make. Just as I had predicted, the snowstorm dissipated. Within 20 minutes, my plane zigzagged through the pass and I landed on Babe Alsworth's lakeside airstrip. Watching my time, I worked until about 3:00 P.M., and then headed back to the Gaede 80 homestead. The plane, like a homing pigeon, could probably have flown home alone; the flight was uneventful.

Descending to about 5,000 feet over the inlet, I started to pick up light turbulence. As I buzzed the house at 4:00 P.M., I knew Ruby would recognize the sound of my plane, and as usual, give a sigh of relief. Then, remembering how Mark had walked in white-faced and silent after making a road landing yesterday, I doubted if she would feel truly relieved until she saw me taxi to my tie-downs.

As I flew over the house, I noted the windsock showed 10 to 15 knots, so I decided to make one more go-around before my final approach. I had never landed the 180 from this direction before, and the road strip left no room for error. Passing over the house, I saw Ruby's father, 88-year-old Solomon Leppke, slowly walking toward the circle drive and supposed he wanted to see me land. I proceeded toward the south end of the angled road. Coming in above the 120-foot trees and easily clearing the power lines over the road, I chopped the engine, expecting to glide about 100 feet.

Suddenly, there was no air to hold me! The plane dropped like a rock, my left wing clipped the tops of the 15-foot spruce trees flanking the road. I made an off-balance touchdown, but the confrontation of my leading edge with the one-inch-diameter trees had pulled the aircraft to the left, and I found myself heading directly toward Roger's newly painted 172! Terrified, I slammed the throttle forward in a desperate attempt to re-establish airspeed, but the 180 had a lag and took precious seconds to respond.

From years of flying, my mind made instant reflex decisions. I evaluated the parameters of heavy wires, trees, and planes—all around me. Frantically I manuevered the yoke at 45 mph, barely missing the guy wires of the light pole. Then, miraculously I leap-frogged both Roger's 172 and my Super Cub. Time moved in slow motion as I headed toward our front yard. As I'd cleared the Cub, the 180 gained an altitude of about 20 feet. At this point, I severed our telephone line with the propeller. The aircraft was really floundering now.

After surviving the Maule wreck, I knew it was possible to survive a controlled crash at a low altitude with a slow speed. But, with my airspeed near stalling and with full power, the prop torque kept me from gaining control. Trees were beside me and electric wires above me. I was living a recurring nightmare, familiar to all bush pilots—the panicked feeling of being boxed in. Suddenly my left wing hit a birch, tearing off five feet of wingtip. My ailerons went with it. I was now above the front lawn.

Later my family told me what they experienced in their ringside seats. Ruby, hearing the sound of a plane aborting landing, rushed from the kitchen to the picture window in our living room, which now served as an enormous television screen portraying a horrifying plot. There was no way to turn off what she saw hurtling over the lawn. Solomon Leppke stood on the edge of the drive. The odd free-form flight of my disoriented bird coming at him stopped him in his tracks. Roger, hearing the scream of my plane in trouble, jumped into his truck and raced to our front road.

Meanwhile, with only ten feet of altitude, I still had hope that I could get around the small grove of trees and return to the road. I had to disengage myself from this bizarre steeplechase! I calculated that if I could pull to the right, I could make it out the driveway, dodge my parked J-3, and bring the plane to a stop—without crashing. My airspeed had dropped to stall, and my damaged wingtip and aileron made control impossible. Then I saw the massive telephone pole loom up right in the way of my intended escape route. My choices were gone. I opted for the trees and chopped the engine.

The plane tore down a four-foot fence, hit one tree, and then smashed into four others, where it rested near the chicken house. The sounds of my bruised black and blue aircraft ended in deathly silence.

Ruby dashed out of the house. As a bush pilot's wife, fears of plane crashes continually lurked in her mind. As Ruth said later, "We'd always expected Dad to have another plane wreck, but we thought it would be across the inlet, not in our front yard."

When Ruby neared the chicken pen, where the plane now roosted, she saw that a wheel was ripped off, both cabin doors were torn away, and the windshield was popped loose, letting univited spruce branches into the cabin. Unaware of the blood dripping from my head, I climbed out of the plane, stunned and amazed that I was still alive. "I'm okay," I said.

"You're not okay," she protested. "You're bleeding. You cut your head."

"I'm all right!" I loudly claimed. In hysterical relief we argued.

Mishal, who had been in Soldotna and missed the drama, drove up to her A-frame across the road from the main house and ambled up the cirular drive. Unaware of the plane lodged in the chicken pen, yet sensing something out of the ordinary, she casually asked, "What happened?"

In confusing parts of sentences, we all tried to explain.

Meanwhile, Roger abandoned his efforts to find my plane and in bewilderment drove up the circular drive, right past the well-camouflaged plane, which hid in the woods like a wounded animal. My family clustered around me.

Conscious now of the warm blood running down the side of my face, and after Mishal's examination of both the three-inch and four-inch gashes in my head, I allowed myself to be taken to the emergency room. At least the shoulder harness had saved my face. Thirty stitches later, Mishal drove me home. I saw the litter-strewn pathway of my kamakaze landing.

Before retiring to the house for the evening, I picked my way back to my plane. Poking my head inside the doorless cabin, I saw several strands of gray hair caught on a protruding screw and gently fluttering in the air. It had been a close call.

For months, I would question other pilots about what I should have done. They all agreed that there were no other options and no "if onlys." They also agreed that gray hair comes with the territory. With deep gratitude, I thanked God for being in control of an out-of-control situation. My number was not up.

No, March 3, 1984, was no ordinary day.

24
The Valley of 10,000 Smokes revisited
August 1986

My appointment book calendar showed a series of crossed out days falling beneath one another on Friday after Friday. Knowing the capriciousness of Alaskan weather, I'd booked off consecutive Fridays in hopes of finding one long weekend to fly to the Valley of 10,000 Smokes—located across the Cook Inlet and to the southwest near King Salmon. So far, the only thing the crossed off Fridays indicated was a long spell of unhealthy flying conditions around King Salmon.

In the spring, I'd remarked to Leonard Olson, "July would

be a great month to go over to the Valley of 10,000 Smokes. The sockeye salmon will be running in the Brooks River, and we'll have endless daylight hours for flying over there and back."

"Whenever you say the word, I'll be ready," replied Leonard, nodding his balding head in enthusiasm.

I'd chosen Leonard, a retired school principal and long-time acquantaince, to be my partner for this trip. With his flexible schedule, he could accompany me at nearly a moment's notice, and he also had an interest in geology and ecology. You have to understand—the Valley of 10,000 Smokes is no typical wilderness area, nor is it a common arctic landform. And, unlike most of my treks around Alaska, this would not be a hunting trip, nor was it an excursion into a village to perform medical duties.

Situated within the Katmai National Park and Preserve, the Valley of 10,000 Smokes was the site of one of the most violent volcanic eruptions in history. In June 1912, Novarupta Volcano (meaning "newly erupted") exploded with a blast of hot wind and gas. Spewing immense quantities of glowing pumice and ash over the terrain, the volcano buried more than 40 square miles of dense green valley. Some of these lava deposits were in depths of 700 feet. Several years after this cataclysmic event, Dr. Robert Griggs, an explorer from the National Geographical Society, named the ash-filled valley with countless steam fumaroles "The Valley of 10,000 Smokes."

As I looked forward to exploring this wonder of the Alaskan world, July came and went, and the Friday weather pattern of IFR conditions, high winds and severe turbulence camped out in the King Salmon area. Meanwhile, my desire to fly to the Valley of 10,000 Smokes grew into an obsession. Restlessly, I crossed off the first Friday in August. Daily, I watched the weather. Even though I knew better than to push into foul weather, even though there were plenty of other fair-weather places to explore, something inside of me urged me on. Finally, on August 15, my routine Friday noon call to FAA gave me the green light. King Salmon had clear skies.

Immediately, I picked up the phone and dialed Leonard. "All systems are go! I'll meet you out at Longmare Lake." I traveled light. It didn't take me long to race home and grab necessities. Just as I'd crawled back into a plane after my first crackup with the Maule, I was soon back up in the air after my

The Valley of 10,000 Smokes revisited   181

unexpected flight into the chicken house. This time, I was in a white with blue trim Super Cub, which depending on the time of year, had floats, wheels, or skis. At the moment, it was on floats.

On my drive to the lake, my mind turned to the first trip I'd taken to the Valley of 10,000 Smokes thirty years ago. That time, my origination point was Lake Hood in Anchorage. That first adventure in the J-3 was shared with Paul Carlson, who had since that time grown into a lifelong friend.

"How would you like to go with me to see the fabulous Valley of 10,000 Smokes?" I'd asked him one night as I poured over flight charts.

"Sure, lead the way," he had chuckled.

Unlike this trip, I didn't remember that one taking so long to move from idea into actuality. But finally it was happening—we were going. The clear blue sky on that late summer day had offered no hint of trouble to come, and the green light from the tower at Lake Hood had given us a cheery send-off.

Now it was a quiet day and the Cub rocked easily on the lake in front of a friend's house. Leonard was waiting and quickly we assembled our gear. As I pulled the floatplane up on the "step," I thought of my first flying lessons as a young and exuberant Kansas farm boy. Then as an inexperienced adventure-seeker I'd had hopes and dreams of exploring the remote Alaskan territory. Since then, little by little and with plane after plane, I'd carved air pathways into this great land.

Just as on my first trip, I crossed over the aquamarine Cook Inlet, now dotted with oilwell platforms, and turned into Lake Clark Pass. I'd traveled this pass numerous times and I respected its propensity for formidable weather. Chills went down my spine as I recalled my "faith flight" following Jack, and I was glad for smooth, dry air on this trip.

It wasn't long before we splashed down on Lake Clark where I had aviation fuel stored at our house there. From there, we continued on, over Illiamna Lake and straight toward Brooks Camp in the Katmai National Park on Naknek Lake. As we neared our destination, the late afternoon sun reflected off the windswept sandy lava floor in sparkling hues of yellow, gold, and light brown.

Within moments, the floats skimmed over the quiet water before settling down and gliding toward the smooth beach. "A perfect day and a perfect landing." I commented to Leonard.

"Yes, and look how close we are to the campsites—no more than a 100 feet away," he said.

The park ranger, a smiling young woman with a round flat-brimmed hat, walked down the beach and filled us in on the pleasures and problems of camping there. "There are about 28 campsites which you can see are well cleared and level." She pointed a short distance away. "There are three shelters for eating and drying out wet clothing. And over there are two food caches. This summer we had 24 brown bear enjoying our river, but now since the main run of salmon have already spawned, only three remain."

The caches with metal ladders stood on skinny legs about 10 feet above the ground, making it impossible for a bear to have a midnight snack.

After pitching our tent, we walked over to the Visitor's Center to attend a slide and film presentation of the Katmai National Park. "Earthquakes had warned the villagers along the Katmai coast of the impending danger and many had fled their homes," the narrator told us. "But even with these precautions, many were caught in ashy darkness for three days and nights while the volcano hurled out the hot debris. At Kodiak, 100 miles southeast of the eruption, the 60 hours of darkness was so complete that a lantern held at arm's length could scarcely be seen."

"I can't wait for the guided tour tomorrow," I whispered to Leonard.

Before returning to our campsite, another pilot found me and advised me to move my plane from the bay into a sheltered spot in the Brooks River. "Frequently, sudden winds come up, which can easily damage a plane."

The bright moon, which was just now climbing up among the stars in the clear sky, seemed to deny such a possibility; nevertheless we moved the plane, then called it a night and slept soundly until a splashing noise awakened us. I reached for my glasses and poked my head out of the tent. "Looks like it's breakfast time—at least for that bear," I said, watching the bear slap a salmon with his enormous paw and then rip it in half with his massive jaws.

"I doubt that we're invited to his salmon buffet," replied Leonard.

We broke camp, carried our belongings to the plane, and headed over to the main lodge for our tour. While we waited,

The Valley of 10,000 Smokes revisited   183

we looked over the rest of the facilities. There were 16 modern guest cabins with eating facilities in the lodge. In a brochure, we read about the numerous fishing and sightseeing trips available for the nearly 4,000 people who had visited here over the past year. Several small planes flew in daily from King Salmon. I remembered calling this a fishing paradise when Paul Carlson and I had caught rainbow and grayling trout, which were hitting the flies.

Two eight-passenger, four-wheel-drive vans pulled up in front of the lodge. Each was equipped with front-end wenches and cable hooks in the rear. One of the drivers noticed our interest and explained. "We always drive together in case of vehicle trouble when we cross the rivers."

Eagerly we climbed into the vans, which started down a very narrow one-way dirt road. We twisted through heavily timbered woods where most of the trees were 40-foot white spruce. Spongy caribou moss and dark moss berries carpeted the forest floor. Crowding together on this cushion were tangled alders, dense willows, and aspen. On several occasions, the buses stopped and let us off to hike over to scenic lookouts or tumbling waterfalls.

By noon, we completed the 23-mile drive and arrived at a Park Service cabin, sitting on top of Overlook Mountain on the edge of the spectacular Valley of 10,000 Smokes. The sun shone brightly over the expansive 14-mile-long 5-mile-wide valley. "We couldn't asked for a better dining view," I said to Leonard as we ate our sack lunches.

"This is the third day like this during this summer," the driver-guide announced.

Visualizing the row of crossed off Fridays on my calendar, I could believe what he said.

"It is thought that, in the 1912 eruption, when four cubic miles of molten rock were ejected from the Novarupta vent, it drained a connecting underground 'plumbing' system to the Katmai magma reservoir so that the Katmai dome collapsed," our guide started to lecture. "This formed the Katmai Caldera and Lake, which have been slowly filling with water at the rate of about 6 to 35 feet per year. Some people believe that the lake will be filled by 2020."

We finished our lunches, took pictures, and continued listening to the guide. "Even though upon the first exploration the valley was called 'The Valley of 10,000 Smokes,' it was later recognized as really being steam instead of smoke. Someone has speculated that this misnomer probably comes from the difficulty some of the native villagers had in saying 'steam' as compared to the ease of saying 'smoke.'

I glanced over at Leonard, who listened with rapt attention. "There are about 20 spots where the fumaroles make wet spots in the sand."

"It seems inconceivable that heat could be stored in the lava for 74 years," I said, nudging Leonard.

"Originally, the fumaroles were up to about 900 degrees celsius," the guide kept his lecture going. "Cooled by the rain and snow, the heat has dissipated."

"We can vouch for the rain," said one of two weary and bedraggled backpackers, who had just climbed up from the valley floor. "We spent over half our time in our tent because of either rain or high winds—there is no protection out there."

We left them as they were hanging their damp shirts over tree limbs and hiked 1½ miles down to the valley floor. Orange, yellow, and blue altered pumice marked the fumaroles, which had at one time criss-crossed the Valley floor. The abrasive combination of tumbling rocks and pumice, water and high winds had eroded a river and canyons. The guide referred to these canyons, which were a couple hundred feet wide, as the "mini Grand Canyon." A mile from the base of the sandblasted Valley, a small amount of green vegetation was starting to heal the lava burns and brighten the lunar-looking terrain. Horsetail and deep pink fireweed sprouted in nooks and crannies.

All too soon, we were told to hike back up to the vans, and by early evening we were back in the sky. "I never would have believed that Alaska had such a place," commented Leonard as we circled around an island-studded lake before heading back home. The often turbulent skies were peaceful, with only a minor crosswind.

"The first time I came here it was a real surprise to me, too." I said, feeling immensely satisfied that I'd had the opportunity to revisit this unique area.

That hadn't been the only surprise on that first trip, though. Suddenly the winds had picked up between King Salmon and Lake Illiamna, tossing the frail J-3 about like a rat in a mad dog's jaws. My camera had flown around in the cabin, as did some of the fishing gear. Paul had attempted to anchor himself to the seat and at the same time secure the identifiable flying objects.

Meanwhile, I had been busy at the few controls the J-3 offered. By calculating our ground speed I had soon realized we were having 50-knot winds at 2,000 feet. With this kind of opposition, we would be marginal on gas to reach a refueling place. I had searched the lakes nearby for a respite until the winds subsided. Thirty years ago, I had been inexperienced in judging emergency situations and chose a lake for its length, not for its smooth surface. From my perspective, the waves did not appear dangerous, so innocently I had set the plane down on the water.

Before I had realized what was happening, the waves had violently shook the plane and large white caps had pounded at the floats. I had idled the engine and turned around to discuss the situation with Paul. As soon as I turned my head, I had seen the impending danger. Out the back side window I saw that the wind was shoving us toward the beach. This was no smooth beach, but one stacked with enormous boulders. Within moments our plane would be pounded to pieces by these giants. "We've got to get out of here or we'll be crushed!" I had yelled to Paul.

I had jammed the throttle forward and pulled back slightly on the stick. The prop wash and the wave spray had completely covered my windshield. Blindly I had tried to feel my way back onto the "step" as the plane floundered in the troughs of rough water. I could feel the waves crest and break as I had continued to ease the stick back. I had hoped to bounce clear of the ensuing waves and increase airspeed and at the same time prevent the plane from stalling. With one gigantic bounce the windshield had cleared and we were airborne.

When we were securely back in the air, I had once again turned back to Paul. "We'll have to fight out this storm up here and hope to make it to Illiamna for gas."

Obviously, that first flight to and from the Valley of 10,000 Smokes ended successfully—probably much like this one, where Lake Clark Pass graciously let us back out over Cook Inlet into a peaceful sky of golden-edged pink clouds.

After thirty years of flying these skies and exploring the Last Frontier, the Alaska fever still lingered in my veins. Even though I'd become familiar with much of the vast land, I was not bored. I still believed there was more adventure to be had and more beauty to be seen—and I fully expected to make more stories.

If anyone asked me, I'd say that the prescription for excitement is living in Alaska.

* * *

Dr. Elmer E. Gaede went to be with Jesus on October 6, 1991. His death was sudden and he is missed by all who knew him.